P$YCHING OUT VEGAS:

WINNING THROUGH PSYCHOLOGY IN THE CASINOS OF THE WORLD

by

MARVIN KARLINS, Ph.D.

A Gambling Times Book
Distributed by Carol Publishing Group

Library of Congress Cataloging in Publication Data
KARLINS, MARVIN
P$YCHING OUT VEGAS

ISBN: 0-914314-03-3

Manufactured in the United States of America

First Carol Publishing Group Edition 1990

Distributed by Carol Publishing Group
120 Enterprise Avenue
Secaucus, NJ 07094

Carol Publishing Group books are available at special discounts
for bulk purchases, for sales promotions, fund raising, or
educational purposes. Special editions can also be created to
specifications. For details contact: Special Sales Department,
Carol Publishing Group, 120 Enterprise Ave., Secaucus, NJ   07094

All material presented in this book is offered as information to the reader. No inducement to gamble is intended or implied.

DEDICATION

TO MY WIFE: Who understood when the chips were down.

CONTENTS

FOREWORD

How Las Vegas P$ychs You Into Losing

If you want to win a psychological battle, it helps to know the tactics and strategy of your opponent. *P$YCH-ING OUT VEGAS* will show you how the Las Vegas casino operators try to psych you into losing . . . and tell you what you can do to beat them at their own game.

P$YCHING OUT VEGAS teaches highly technical methods that will help you turn your gambling into a profitable business venture, how to bet, and where to bet.

After you've learned all about how casinos are set up to defeat you, you will then find out how to turn the dealers into much-needed friends, rather than foes. *P$YCHING OUT VEGAS* even takes you as far as to show you how to implement various personality changes to cover up the fact they are professional gamblers conducting a business that is designed to beat the casino.

There is even a section entitled "A Personal Note to the Degenerate Gambler." Reading this will most certainly help you evaluate for yourself whether or not you are a compulsive gambler whom, perhaps, would be better off staying away from Las Vegas and all other towns like it.

Whenever you go to Vegas, you can look forward to the experience—not just in terms of winning, but also as an opportunity to sharpen your psychological strength against the juggernaut casinos.

Winning the psychological battle against the dream merchants is important. It gives you the psychological advantage not only in the casinos, but anywhere that mental power is needed. As strange as it may seem, a casino is an excellent place to develop mental resolve, to learn psychological self-control under fire. After all, if you can resist the temptations of Las Vegas...What mountain can't you climb?

The next time you hit Vegas, plunge into the psychological fray with all guns blazing! Gain the psychological edge and you'll have your gambling chance of winning...in all of life's little games.

P$YCHING OUT VEGAS

CHAPTER 1

BEYOND THE "JAWS OF AVERAGES"

> "Ever wonder why I'm still
> dealing a game that can be
> beat? Because percentages
> aren't the whole story.
> There's the mental factor. I
> don't care how well a player
> can count cards...if he can
> be psyched out, he's gonna
> end up a loser. In this town
> they figure you'll lose your
> shirt once you lose your
> head."
> —*Las Vegas Blackjack Dealer*

Let me share with you my favorite Las Vegas story. It isn't fiction. I was there when it happened.

1

Las Vegas On $60,000 a Day

It was my second day on a junket and things weren't going my way. I was in a posh Strip casino, exhorting two plastic cubes to come up with the point number 5. They weren't listening. "Seven...line away, pay the *don'ts*," intoned the stickman, and a sure-handed dealer whisked my chips off the green baize layout.

It was then that "Mr. C" made his appearance at the table. He was wearing an old pair of soiled pants and a denim work shirt and, as he edged up to the rail, he looked like an auto mechanic ready to shoot a little craps on his lunch break. He took some crumpled bills from his shirt pocket and called for twenty nickel ($5.00) chips. The stickman shoved six dice in his direction and announced: "New shooter coming out." I eyed the unkempt "Mr. C," and decided he looked as frayed as my bankroll. I took it as a sign and decided it was time to take a break.

A few hours later, I was walking past the casino when I heard the unmistakable clamor of gamblers at a hot table. A winning table is a noisy table...and a crowded one. Players shout out bets and cheer the shooter, while spectators push and shove to catch a glimpse of the game. By the time I reached the scene, people were stacked up three-deep around the table, and I had to strain just to get a glimpse of the action. It was a big game. Lots of black ($100) chips dotted the layout. The players were hunched over the table like hungry wolves over a freshly-killed carcass; now, however, they were feasting on the casino's chips—frantically doled out by harried dealers as number after number kept showing on the dice.

And who was at the center of all the tumult? None other than the slovenly "Mr. C." This time, however, I hardly noticed his dress; far more imposing was the groove-full of black chips in front of him. It was hard to believe. There must have been $20,000 there!

I watched "Mr. C" play. He was a *"desperado"*—a Vegas term for a gambler who likes to bet fast and hard. When a good hand shows, a *desperado* can take the casino for a bundle. When the dice are cold...well, a *desperado* doesn't stay around very long. The dice stayed hot. "Mr. C" ran out of rail space to store his chips, and he began stuffing the overflow in his two shirt pockets. As the dice kept passing, he began to bulge noticeably in the chest area, giving the appearance of a female impersonator with a lumpy bra. It was really quite comical, but nobody was laughing, particularly the pit boss who realized the padding represented about $10,000 worth of house money.

I observed the game a while more, until the dice started chopping, and players drifted from the table. "Mr. C" showed no signs of quitting, and I wondered if he'd have the good sense to pull in his horns and take down a profit. I made a mental note to check back at the tables after I took in dinner and a show.

The next time I saw "Mr. C" was five hours later. He was still at the same crap table, tossing black chips onto the layout from a stack he kept cupped in his right hand. His shirt pockets were still stuffed, and now there were significant bulges in his pants pockets as well. "Mr. C" was literally bloated with casino chips...and his gluttony was not going unnoticed. A security guard kept a knot of curious onlookers a respectable distance from the table, while several floormen and the shift boss watched the action from the dice pit.

I wondered about "Mr. C's" endurance...and his luck. Could either hold out much longer? I overheard a boxman tell a dealer that "Mr. C" had been going nonstop for over nine hours. All that action at high stakes can do funny things to a person's head. I took a closer look. "Mr. C's" movements had slowed a bit and he was drinking steadily; still, he didn't seem to be losing. I remembered Einstein's observation about God playing dice with the universe and wondered if He had designated "Mr. C" to be the shooter.

* * *

Morning is always too early in Las Vegas. I woke up around 11:30 and decided a good deli lunch would shake yesterday's cobwebs out of my mind. I was on my way to the restaurant when I spotted "Mr. C" standing next to his suitcase, just a few feet from the hotel entrance. He was still wearing the same dirty clothes, but his face looked different. There was a strangeness in his eyes. I wondered what had happened.

"You know him?"

The voice caught me by surprise. It was a hotel bellman who had taken my bags on several occasions. "Do you know him?" the bell man repeated.

"Not really...I saw him gambling yesterday," I answered.

"Did you hear what happened to him?"

"No. I was just wondering about that."

The bellman shook his head. "He was winning a lot of money..."

"I know...must've been $40,000."

"More like $60,000. They had to send out the racks to get the chips to the cage."

"He cashed in?"

"Nope. Safekeeping. When he got to $60,000 he decided to take a break."

"To his room...?"

"That's the real joke. He didn't have a room. He was a drifter, passing through..."

"No job?"

"He said he was an unemployed pipefitter from Chicago, going to LA to find work. He stopped off in Vegas as a lark."

"He must've had some money," I interjected, "I saw him buy in for a hundred at the tables."

"That was his whole bankroll...the last hundred bucks to his name."

"That's hard to believe," I said.

"If you think that's hard...wait till you hear the rest of the story." The bellman waved his arms with a flourish. "When the shift boss found out the guy didn't have a room, they gave him the penthouse suite...sent him right up."

"One suitcase and all?" I asked wryly.

"That's not all they sent up there." The bellman gave me a wink.

"Looks like the management didn't want to see 'Mr. C' abscond with his winnings."

"No way," the bellman agreed.

"Go on..."

"Around eight o'clock the guy wakes up and staggers down to the casino. He's still got a hangover and he's walking bowlegged...but he remembers that money and he wants some heavy action. The swing shift was alerted and waiting for him—opened up a new table...the works."

"And he started betting fast and heavy..."

"He couldn't get it down fast enough. He was covering all the numbers and taking the field at a thousand a pop."

"I know...I watched him yesterday."

"Well, yesterday the dice were passing...this morning they weren't."

"Did anybody ever tell you you're quite a philosopher?" I inquired, looking first at the bellman and then at "Mr. C" still camped near the doorway. "How long did it take to break him?"

"An hour. He ran through every cent he had. When he was wiped, they got his bag out of the penthouse, gave him some walking money, and told him to hit the road."

"Did he say anything to anybody?"

"What's there to say," the bellman wondered, shrugging his shoulders. "The man lost $60,000 in an hour. That says it all."

* * *

In a way, my bellman friend was right. What else *could* one say? An unemployed construction worker loses sixty thousand in sixty minutes...maybe more money than he'll see in a lifetime. It's enough to scramble a person's brain. It must have scrambled mine, because suddenly I felt compelled to approach "Mr. C," and solicit his opinions on the matter.

I walked over to where he was standing. "Excuse me..." I said awkwardly, not knowing exactly how to begin. "...Weren't you the guy I saw winning at the tables yesterday?"

"Mr. C" turned and faced me directly. "Yes. But I just finished losing it all back." There was no rancor in his voice, not even a hint of disappointment. He sounded matter-of-fact, like some anchorman reporting the six o'clock news.

"All of it? You must have been winning thousands of dollars."

6

"All of it . . . $62,500 to be exact."

I couldn't understand how he could be so nonchalant. "My God, man. What happened? Why didn't you put some of it away?"

"Mr. C" stared at me with his strange blue eyes. They were wide and unmoving. "I wanted action."

Something about that response irritated me, and I snapped back: "Action? But for what? Now you have zero . . . you have nothing to show for it."

My outburst didn't seem to have any effect. "You're wrong," he countered. "I do have something to show for it."

"Oh, yeah? What?"

"Memories." A wisp of a smile played across "Mr. C's" face. *"I've got memories to show for it."* And without a further word, the unemployed pipefitter from Chicago picked up his suitcase, walked out the hotel door, and disappeared into the simmering heat of the Las Vegas afternoon.

Paradise with a Pair-A-Dice?

Let me guess what you're thinking. You're thinking that "Mr. C" was crazy. "How could anybody be so stupid?" you're wondering. Yet, the amazing thing is that every year millions of Las Vegas visitors drop millions of dollars at the tables. They, too, walk away happy, cherishing the memories of their trip while seemingly oblivious to the carnage enacted upon their bankrolls. Granted, most of them didn't gamble as high or recklessly as "Mr. C," but they *did* lose and they *did* leave savoring fond memories. Most can't wait to return for another plucking. Why?

7

Because the "marks" were "cooled out," folks. Which is Con Man jargon for saying that the visiting gamblers ("marks") were separated from their funds in a manner that left them feeling satisfied with the outcome ("cooled out"). Remember how Tom Sawyer got all those neighborhood kids to whitewash his fence? Those kids even paid him to do it, because he psyched them into believing it was an enjoyable job. Now *that* was cooling out the mark. The pharmaceutical company that produces cherry flavored cough syrup also understands the importance of cooling out the mark. And the casino operator who creates an environment that makes losers feel like winners does, too.

Which brings us to a fine irony: every day gamblers from all over the world pour into Nevada in search of the golden fleece . . . and every day most of them return home—victims of the golden fleecing . . . Las Vegas style. The fleece-seeker has become the fleeced with nary a whimper, bedazzled by the Vegas "sleight-of-mind."

Sound ridiculous? Believe me, it isn't! Las Vegas has been skillfully designed to mollify losers—to cool them out and make them feel their losses were "worth it." That these losers keep coming back is proof-positive Vegas "works."

Of course, to keep losers coming back, one must have losers in the first place. To stimulate losing, Las Vegas has been expertly designed to encourage spending ("splurging") rather than saving . . . *losing rather than winning*. Put another way, Vegas has been designed to *psych you out* of your money, to make you more ready, willing and likely to lose your bankroll at the tables.

You've heard of a Venus Fly Trap and what it does. Well, think of Las Vegas that way . . . as a "Vegas Fly Trap." The whole town is a highly sophisticated money trap, created to separate you from your funds with

elegance, efficiency and *elan*. Do you think it's an accident that you must walk through the casino on your way
into the hotel or to a show? Or that you must cash
checks at the casino cage rather than at the registration
desk? Or that chips (rather than cash) are used at the
tables? Or that players are plied with free drinks while
gaming? No, sir! The Nevada economy prospers because
gambling towns create and encourage a "blow it all"
mentality. Nor should the casino operators or town
fathers be criticized for their approach. They're in the
business of gambling—and encouraging people to hold
on to their money is not good business.

Well then, what about you, the guy or gal who wants a
gambling chance of winning in the casino? Your goal
should be to turn the tables on Vegas: to beat the casino
operators at their own psychological games, and gain
that all-important mental edge. And it becomes my job
as a gambler and a psychologist to share with you the
strategy for accomplishing this goal. First this involves
showing you how Las Vegas psychs you into losing.
Simply understanding these various casino ploys will
put you in a better position to fight and overcome them.
Then we can examine how *you* can psych out Las
Vegas . . . and win.

They Don't Call It "Lost Wages," Nevada For Nothing

Gaining the mental edge in Vegas will be a formidable
challenge. Be warned: "The professional casino operators
are among the most astute practical psychologists in existence today."[1] They understand every nuance of human
emotion and weakness; they know every psychological
trick to get the player to turn his pants pockets inside
out—the gambler's white flag of surrender. But victory

can be yours—it *can* be achieved—and *must be* if you
want to build profits rather than casinos in Las Vegas.

CHAPTER 2

THE DREAM MERCHANTS

"Vegas casinos have a mist-like,
fairytale quality about them...
You are a sleeping beauty waiting
for the prince of good fortune. It
is not too important that your
pockets are being emptied while
you dream. You are glad to pay
the price. You may even feel you
are getting a bargain. And if you
can win—AH!...But remember,
after three days it all turns
into a pumpkin."
—*Mario Puzo, Inside Las Vegas*

Hey, let's face it...life isn't always the carefree, high-class experience we'd like it to be. There are problems out there; hassles and heartaches, too. "If someone had told me being an adult would be this difficult," a friend once claimed, "I wouldn't have grown up." Unfortunately, no one has yet discovered the fountain of youth; but I suspect there's a little Peter Pan in all of us . . . a touch of childlike spirit that makes us want *Never-Never Land* where we can play all day and never grow up. Perhaps that's why we flock to Disneyworld . . . even when we don't have kids.

Well, let me tell you some good news and some bad news. First the good news: there is now a Disneyworld for adults, a place where your fantasies can become reality. And it's not some dinky little theme park off the Interstate—no sir, this is an entire city where you can leave the woes and cares of the world behind and start L-I-V-I-N-G. Las Vegas is its name, and dream fulfillment is its game. The bad news? If you're not careful your dream could turn into a nightmare . . . and I want to wake you up to that possibility before it happens.

Living In a Dream World

When the typical visitor arrives in Las Vegas, it's like placing a starving man in the middle of a circular banquet table. For three days, maybe four, Mr. or Ms. Average American shifts into a frenetic high gear: eating to excess; staying up to excess; seeing shows to excess; and . . . yes . . . gambling to excess. It's as if something had jolted the concept of moderation right out of their bodies and sent them on a full-throttled roar through the city. They are "wired"—and that's the way they stay until they return home and drag around for several days, victims of "Vegas burnout."

When I lived in Las Vegas, I became accustomed to this frenzied behavior of the tourists. What never ceased to amaze me, however, was the visitors' ignorance over *why* they acted the way they did. Their behavior didn't just "happen" out of the blue...these individuals were psyched up and out by the Las Vegas environment—an environment specifically designed to encourage frantic overindulgence, the kind that leads to drooping eyelids and drained billfolds.

What the Vegas visitor fails to comprehend is that the *whole town* has been carefully and purposefully created as a backdrop for playing out the adult dream of *socially justified* indulgence. The key words here are "socially justified." Under normal circumstances adults who indulge themselves are frowned upon, their behavior viewed as childish and inappropriate. Yet, in Vegas this behavior not only is condoned, it is encouraged as a kind of patriotic civic response. How much can you spend... how long can you party...how big can you gamble: these become measures of self-worth in a town that worships the pursuit of the excessive.

And the visitor is more than happy to prove himself worthy! Placed in an environment that frees him from his inhibitions, he takes off like a pack of hounds turned loose on a fox. "It sure ain't this way back home," becomes his rallying cry, and off he goes on a hedonistic binge while the Vegas dream merchants, our friendly casino operators, cheerfully observe the results of their handiwork.

What they see is what they get...the visitor's bankroll. Which is what they expected to get. After all, the casino management didn't invest time and money creating a fairyland of childlike delights simply to make the visitor's trip a pleasant one. They are hard-nosed businessmen and savvy-practical psychologists. They have created the dream world that is contemporary Las Vegas because they know it will bring in greater casino profits.

How the Dream World Works

When we realize that Las Vegas has been built as a kind of "fantasy island" for acquiring the golden fleece, then the whole crazy city begins to make sense.

For instance, consider its location. When I first came to Vegas I remember thinking it had no right being there. I wondered what demented mentality had decided to build a neon-studded luxury resort in the middle of utter desolation . . . surrounded by scorched desert sand and parched, lifeless mountains.

Yet, in the context of dream construction, it makes ultimate sense. To manipulate people, scientists tell us, just put them in a controlled environment, preferably one that is unfamiliar. Then what better place than the middle of a desert? Far away from anywhere, sealed off from the intrusions of the outer world, strikingly novel . . . a desert location provides an isolated, unique setting where a dream can be created without external interruptions. Put Vegas in the center of the picture . . . and the dream potential really soars. The very sight of such an opulent oasis in the midst of desert desolation produces a surrealistic, dreamlike effect which gets the imagination percolating. At night Vegas becomes a compelling invitation to fantasy. A jewel asparkle in the blue-black darkness . . . it looks every bit like the Promised Land, the pot of gold beyond the rainbow, the end of the yellow brick road.

Putting Vegas in the desert has another advantage, too. It encourages people to gamble more. I mean, what else is there to do in the middle of a town a few miles from Death Valley? The city fathers are well aware that the longer you gamble, the better your chances are of losing. That is why all major activities revolve around the casino (see Chapter 3). In the meantime, keeping you in the casino area is made eminently easier because of the harsh, foreboding environment outside.

Some of the brochures sent out by the Las Vegas Chamber of Commerce make a pitch for all the non-gambling activities in and around the town. Such activities do exist, but Vegas, you remember, is in the *desert*. That means most things worth seeing or doing occur within 500 feet of a casino. *Inside* things...like watching a show, eating a meal, making love, or (if you're staying at a major hotel) participating in some indoor tennis or visiting a health spa.

Some outdoor activities are available, but many of these are seasonal. Sporting facilities, for example, can be used daily during part of the year; but during the long summer months they are wisely avoided by all but a few lunatics who enjoy watching their tennis shoes melt. There is sightseeing, too. Hoover Dam, Death Valley and Mt. Charleston are comfortable one-day excursions, but they're not the kind of trips you'd want to take again and again. One trip that *is* worth repeating is a visit to the Grand Canyon, but it's a long journey by car and most visitors (unless they take the air tour) don't like spending that much time away from the Vegas environs. And that's about it...except for a tour of the desert terrain which, for most people, is not particularly an attention-grabber.

So much for "what to see and do" in and around Vegas. (I'll be including a "full" list of activities in Chapter 16.) If some of you feel my assessment is a bit harsh, remember that Vegas wasn't exactly a high priority vacation spot before big league gambling came to town...and it won't be in the future if the tables ever shut down. Mario Puzo put it succinctly: "There is no reason for the existence of Las Vegas except that it has legalized gambling."[2] And that, gentle readers, is the long and short of it.

The dream merchants of Vegas have used the desert as a kind of subtle, natural boundary, designed to keep you, the visitor, inside the city...close to those temples of temptation known as casinos. It is in those temples that you'll encounter another factor that makes the Vegas dream "work": *stimulus bombardment.*

Anyone who's ever been to Las Vegas will know all about stimulus bombardment. It occurs when a person is confronted with more sights and sounds than he or she is used to handling. Like walking down the Vegas "Strip" with its neon dazzle, or stepping into a casino amidst the din of crapshooters and spinning slots. In Vegas, stimulus bombardment is a way of life and it *cannot be avoided.* This is because the *whole town* is wired to turn you on...and on...and on. Twenty-four non-stop hours a day.[3]

What happens when you're subjected to day after day of constant stimulus bombardment? Scientists know ...and so do the casino owners. You begin to think and act differently. Rational thought becomes more difficult. You become more emotional, more impulsive. Normal defenses and inhibitions seem to melt away. Do you know what that adds up to at the tables? One whopping big "psych-out" against the players.

The Vegas dream, then, has created a tasty recipe for gambler ruin: take a cityfull of stimulus bombardment, mix carefully with one part atmosphere of indulgence, add a generous portion of casino gambling...and rake your victim slowly over the coals!

If you want to make the recipe even more potent, there is an additional ingredient that can be added: a "dash" of party atmosphere. The dream merchants have worked hard to give Vegas the aura of perpetual partying, a kind of 365-days-a-year Mardi Gras. This party atmosphere is crucial to legitimizing socially justified indulgence. After all, isn't that what a party's all about? Let the good times roll! Eat, drink and be merry! Life is a cabaret my friend...so just belly on up to the table and put a black chip on the hardways...what the hell, it's *only* money...and besides, it's *fun*.

There's no room for party-poopers in the manufactured gaiety of the casino. Winners are heralded by the ringing of bells and the shouts of the dealers. Drinks and cigarettes are readily available...free for the asking. Nearby a band is playing happy music...and in the showroom there's a comedian to keep you laughing. This is a world where "...everything goes—it's fast, it's fun, and it's loose, so visitors 'let it all hang out.'"[4] What usually ends up hanging out, however, is the player's pants pockets...the white flag of surrender. Can anything be done about it?

Is There a Way to Keep the Las Vegas Dream From Becoming a Nightmare?

Yes...simply by becoming aware of the ploys that are being used against you, you will be taking a *small* step in the right direction. It will help you see the Vegas environment for what it is...a carefully manufactured dreamworld designed to separate you from your money.

The next time you go to Vegas, do this. Look around you. Observe the stagecraft for what it is. Study the fantasyland the dream merchants have created. Then run like hell to your room and read this statement over and over:

Every dream has it price.   In Disneyworld, they charge you at the entrance. In Vegas, the admission is free...but it costs plenty if you let them take you for a ride.

Again, by becoming aware of the dream merchants' ploys, you will be taking a *small* step in the right direction. It is not a sufficient step, however, to provide strong protection against their manipulations. For that you will need a more powerful defense, more sophisticated techniques to psych out the casino operators and gain the mental edge. In the second half of this book I will be presenting the *major* tools you can use to carve out this psychological victory. First, though, I'd like to introduce you to more of the dream merchants' handiwork...so you will understand *all* the psychological tactics they employ to make you a loser at the tables. So get a firm grip on your bankroll, and let's take a stroll into the center of the Vegas dream.

CHAPTER 3

A WALK INTO THE WEB

"Step into my parlor said the
spider to the fly . . ."
—From A Children's
Nursery tale

"We got 'em once they walk
through the front door."
—Casino Pit Boss

Caesars Palace is a deluxe hotel-casino on the Strip,
aglow like a giant blue ice cube in the Las Vegas night.
Let me tell you an interesting story about the place.

The Strange Case of the One-Way Runway

If you've ever been to the "Palace," you know it is set
back from one of the busiest intersections on the Strip.

It is several hundred yards from the street to the casino door. Now, several hundred yards might not sound like much of a distance to travel . . . but in Vegas, people have been known to evaporate walking from their hotel room to the swimming pool! At any rate, Caesars has constructed a rainbow-shaped "skyway," complete with moving runway, to whisk gamblers from the Strip intersection right to the front door of the hotel.

Recently, I decided to try out the skyway. It was fun. As the trip progressed a recorded voice described all the great pleasures awaiting me as an honored guest of Caesar himself. Well, that was pretty heady stuff . . . and by the time I hit the end of the runway, I was ready to participate in all sorts of debauchery.

I stayed at the Palace for several hours, then decided to visit some downtown casinos. I walked outside and looked for the return runway. There was none. Nowhere. I finally checked with the doorman. "We bring them in, but we don't take them out," was his reply.

*   *   *

The one-way runway at Caesars Palace is important because it tells us something about the Vegas dream merchants and how they think. The guiding principle of the casino operators— and, therefore, the prime directive for all of Vegas—is: *get people into the casinos and keep them there.* Or, as one hotel executive quipped, "Get 'em in and keep 'em in." And that is *exactly* what the one-way runway was built to accomplish. Caesars Palace is happy to provide an expensive transport that will make your access to the casino both easy and attractive. But leaving—well, that's a horse of a different color. At that point you're on your own. Meanwhile, the dream merchants can always hope that once you leave their air conditioned hotel and realize you have to walk back to the

Strip, you'll turn around and head back into their casino.

"Get 'em in and keep 'em in." Now that we're aware of this #1 axiom, a whole lot of things about Vegas makes sense. For instance:

The Casino as Focal Point

Consider, for a moment, the orb-weaving spider. This clever little insect spins a web to trap its prey. Some spiders are smarter than others. The clever ones spin their webs in places where passing meals are more likely to fly by...like around outdoor lights. After all, the better the traffic flow, the better the menu.

Dream merchants build webs, too. Their webs are called "casinos" (guess what role *you* play). And, like the clever spider, they build theirs where traffic density is high. But, whereas the spider can't alter its environment to "draw more customers" into its web (it might search for an outdoor light, but it can't build one), a casino operator can...and does. This is why the casino has become the focal point of Vegas: the city has been designed to funnel more people into the casino web. Want some examples?

ITEM: In most hotels, you have to pass through or along the edge of the casino to get to the front desk.

ITEM: If you want to cash any travelers checks, most establishments direct you to the casino, rather than to the hotel cashier.

ITEM: Getting to and from most shows requires a trip through the casino. And while you're waiting to enter... guess where they have you line up.

ITEM: Spiders build their webs near bright lights because doing so attracts more "customers" at night.

21

Ever notice the candlepower along the Strip, or in casino-center?

ITEM: Most of the hotel dining establishments—particularly the gourmet restaurants—are accessible only by a trip through the casino.

ITEM: Many large hotels limit or refuse to offer activities or services that keep customers away from the casino. For example: "...when the Desert Inn proposed Las Vegas' first eighteen-hole golf course in 1952, the other hotels opposed its development. The Strip resorts did not even put television sets in their rooms until the 1960's."[5] (To this day, many casino-hotels refuse to accept free TV programming guides for distribution in guests' rooms.) Some casino managers don't like efficient room service; they'd rather have the customer eating in the restaurants near the casino.[6]

Nobody should underestimate the importance of the "casino as focal point" concept. I'm sure you've all heard at least one story about a Vegas visitor who ended up gambling because he passed a casino while on his way to somewhere else. Normally, these stories don't have very happy endings. In fact, some of the most memorable tales in gambling folklore attest to the effectiveness of placing casinos at the crossroads to everywhere.

Take, for example, the story of the well known comedian, Joe E. Lewis. It seems he was on a dinner date. When his companion asked for some cigarettes, he excused himself from the table and walked to the lobby newsstand to get a pack. The newsstand, of course, was at the edge of the casino. Joe E. Lewis liked to gamble. A few minutes later he returned and the meal was completed without further interruption. Later, as he prepared to leave the restaurant, he noticed his lady friend had left the cigarettes on the table.

"Better take them with you, honey," he suggested, "they cost me $32,000." And Joe E. Lewis, the comedian, wasn't joking.[7]

Embellishing the Web

The casino owners know their livelihoods depend on gaming revenue. They also know that in the long run a certain proportion of all monies gambled will end up in their coffers. Thus, they have made their casinos the focal point of the city in hopes of getting more action at the tables. And they haven't stopped there. They've even "one-upped" our orb-weaving spider by coming up with a better "web." A spider's web is inconspicuous and does nothing to entice any prey that happens by. Not so with a casino. The Vegas "web" is very carefully designed as a lure, embellished with all kinds of goodies to make it more attractive and irresistible.

Take, for example, the giveaways and drawings that are always available in Vegas. Where are they held? In the casino. You must enter the web to win. There are lounge shows and bars in almost every casino as well, with the music and liquor doing their share of bringing visitors into the web. Then, too, there are the shills—they are usually attractive women—who sit at the gaming tables, adding their presence to an already compelling environment. And, most important, there are the amplified sounds of WINNING—slots buzzing and money clanking into metal bowls...sounds that summon gamblers to the tables as surely as bells call a congregation to Sunday worship.

There are not many individuals who can stand outside the web and resist falling prey to the temptations just a few steps away. Which brings us to the the problem of:

23

Getting People to Stick Around the Casino

What happens when someone walks into the web? Our friendly spider makes sure any visitor stays put by making his web a sticky one. And so do the dream merchants who, you will remember, want to "get you in and *keep you in*" ("the longer that you stay, the longer you might play").

Keeping people in casinos is not that difficult—particularly when you consider the other activities available in the desert. Then, too, the lures that drew a person to the casino in the first place—money, women, music, etc. —can also help hold him there. In addition, the casino operators provide extra "adhesives" once you enter the casino; for instance, they dangle "fun books" that offer free rolls of nickels, two-for-one play at various table games, even souvenirs. The hitch? You have to check in every hour at a casino booth. It is literally impossible to leave the casino and still use the books. So you stay in the web. The casino management also makes sure there are no clocks around to remind the player of any other commitments. Time is literally suspended in the casinos. And they never close, so there is no time limit requiring the casinos to arbitrarily cut off play (whoever heard of a spider turning out a fly because it was closing time!).

Gambling: the Ultimate Adhesive

However, the *best way* to keep a person in a casino is...gambling itself. Once a person starts, it is hard for him to stop—at least while money is still available to put into action. It is this compelling, addictive aspect of gambling that makes it the singlemost powerful adhesive for keeping you in the casino.

Some of the things people will go through to keep gambling are almost beyond belief. If you doubt the addictive power of gambling, consider these *true* stories:

★ A few years back there was a flash flood that roared through Vegas. Water surged into the casino at Caesars Palace, and stood several feet deep in places. It didn't stop the gamblers. They just rolled up their pants and kept shooting craps!

★ A fire burned through part of a large Strip hotel. Even as smoke curled through the casino, gamblers were reluctant to leave. The slot players were a particular problem. One woman steadfastly refused to leave her machine, and she had to be carried bodily from the burning building.

★ A man had a heart attack while shooting craps. He was laid out on the casino carpet, in full view of the other players, to await an ambulance. The game never stopped for a moment.

★ A friend of mine was also shooting dice. He had been playing for several hours when he felt the urge to visit the bathroom. Just then the dice turned hot. They stayed that way. My friend had a choice: stay on the hot roll and defecate in his pants; or go the the bathroom and interrupt his winning streak. He crapped in his pants. Now I know how the game got its name.

Now, here's something to remember. The people in the stories I have just recounted were not hardcore, degenerate gamblers...they were typical Vegas visitors, the kind who pour into the city day after day. *People like you.* Yet—caught up in the fever pitch of gambling—they did some very strange things. And some not-very-strange things—like losing money. Why? Because they succumbed to the casino's temptations;

they were psyched out.

Learn to Walk Through the Web

Here's one last interesting fact about spider webs. Certain spiders can walk on them yet not get stuck. The same is true of casino "webs." Some can walk into the web, have a good time, and walk out again. Others get stuck. . . figuratively and financially.

By now you are aware that ". . .the casino atmosphere has been designed by experts. . .to color your judgment and to make winning more difficult."[8] You also know that the casino owners will do everything possible to get you into the casino and keep you there. If you want to emerge a winner, you must enter only when you're psychologically ready (not on a "whim"), and learn to leave before you overextend your billfold. Section II of this book will show you how to walk the web unscathed. For now, I just want you to be aware of the Vegas webs: why they are there and how they work.

CHAPTER 4

CASINO COMPS:
THE FREE LUNCH AS A LAST MEAL

"My last trip to Vegas was
free...the casino picked up
all the costs. All I had to pay
was my gambling losses."
—*Las Vegas Junket Gambler*

Here's a question for you. What was your favorite holiday when you were a kid? I'll tell you mine: it was Halloween. And you know why? It wasn't the costumes...or even staying out late at night. It was the concept of "trick or treat." Not so much the candy itself. Hell, I could buy candy any time I wanted. It was the idea of *free* candy...as much as I cared to collect. Just walk up to a door, hold our your bag, and presto—a free handout! Oh, the delight of it all!

If you can understand my fascination for Halloween, and if you share my attitude about getting things free, then you're going to love Las Vegas. Because, in Las

Vegas, Halloween is an everyday affair.

In America, the land of the free, Las Vegas is the land of the freebie.

Pick up any copy of the free Vegas tabloids from the racks which proliferate along the sidewalks and street corners. Inside there are enough free offer coupons to make a Halloween bag go limp with envy. Free meals. Free fun books. Free drawings and giveaways. Free drinks. Even free photos of you standing next to a million dollars or a professional gambler.

Of course, some freebies aren't available to everyone. For instance, free meals are available to anybody who turns in a coupon . . . but only a few individuals can spend time with an attractive call girl free of charge.

What kind of freebies can *you* expect to get? That all depends on what kind of gambler you are. If you gamble for long periods of time and bet big amounts of money you can expect some real nice freebies. If you gamble recklessly, all the better. So you see, some Vegas "freebies" aren't really free after all . . . but more on that later.

If you're a real "high roller," they'll give you the keys to the city. Take, for example, the case of one big spender who had a high credit limit at the casino. The hotel picked up his air fare to and from Las Vegas, plus his room, food, and beverage bills. The player was pleased but he wanted to see how much the hotel cared for him. So he requested that a young lady be sent to his room for a little companionship. The request was granted. Then he asked that a different lady be sent up on each subsequent night. Again, the hotel complied with his wishes. Not quite sure the hotel *really* cared for him, he let it be known that he desired two partners for the coming evening. Again, his request was honored.

Totally exhausted, by the next morning he no longer doubted the hotel's affection for him.[9]

Junkets: The Ultimate Freebie

In movies, you've made it if you get an Oscar. In science, you're tops if you win the Nobel Prize. And in the world of Las Vegas freebies, you've reached the pinnacle if you're invited on a "junket."

Not all junkets are the same. Some are better than others, meaning some give away more and better freebies than others. But, basically, if you've got between $5,000-$7,500 you're willing to put into action at the tables, here's the kind of freebie package you can expect: a four or five-day stay in Vegas, free roundtrip air fare, plus an "RFB comp"—room, food and beverage, compliments of the sponsoring hotel-casino.

If you don't have that much to risk—say your budget is more like $2,000—then you might end up on a "mini-junket." Mini-junkets are usually one or two-day trips, often with less "freebie-frills" once you arrive. At the other end of the scale, if you've got $10,000 or more to play with, things can really get interesting: first-class air fare, the privilege of bringing along a guest for free, a palatial suite at the sponsoring hotel, gourmet everything, free shows, and transportation while you're in town. (Please keep in mind that the money requirements for junkets change to keep pace with inflation.)

How Do You Get on a Junket?

It's easy (maybe *too* easy). Junkets to Vegas fly out of every major city in the country. To go, all you need is a

29

healthy bank account (a sizeable amount of money in your *checking* account helps greatly), excellent credit, and a few postage stamps. Write to the various Las Vegas hotels where you might want to stay, and inquire about junkets flying from your city. Address your letter in care of the casino manager. Then get ready to pack your bags . . . you'll be getting replies sooner than you think (Las Vegas is always looking for new high rollers). If you want to avoid the letter-writing hassle, try checking around your area for the names of some junket representatives—you'd be surprised how many people know about junkets and who runs them. You might even try calling your local travel agency, as travel representatives often know the names of junket organizers in the area. In fact, some junkets are run out of travel agencies.

Once it has been established that you have adequate financial resources, you'll receive a junket invitation. If it is your first junket to Vegas, you'll oftentimes be required to put some money "up front." This front money is deposited with the casino when you arrive, and you draw on it by signing markers at the tables when you begin gambling. The reason that front money is required of new players is to reduce the risk of junket "free-loaders"—people who attend junkets but have no intention of gambling. (Vegas has had problems with these freeloaders. When you consider that the hotel has to lay out $1,000 or more per person on a five-day junket, you can see the financial burden such people create.)

Once you have established your credibility as a "serious" player, the front money requirement will usually be dropped, and the casino will extend you credit, just as banks do with your Visa or Mastercharge cards. The amount of that credit (called your credit limit) will be based on how much you request and your financial worth. You can then play against your credit line at the tables—which means you don't have to bring money out to Vegas with you. If, at the end of a junket, you come out ahead...then you take your winnings home with you. If you finish up "in the hole," you are allowed to either write a check to cover your loss, or pay your debt off once you return home. The length of time they might give a player to settle a gambling debt varies with the casino, the particular junket, and the player's "value" to the hotel. Normally, the more a casino values your business, the longer you can take to pay off what you owe.

At this point I'd like to clarify an issue that often confuses prospective junket-goers. When a casino requires $5,000 for a front money deposit or credit line in order for you to attend a junket, it is *not* requiring the player to lose the $5,000. The casino is only asking that you will be willing to *risk that amount of money in action at the tables*. Whether you win or lose really makes no difference to them. As I pointed out earlier, the casino owners play the percentages: they know a certain proportion of monies gambled will, in the long run, end up in their hands. A casino executive might put it this way to the player: "We're willing to spend some money on you, if you're willing to give us a reasonable shot at your bankroll." Can anyone really deny that such a request is reasonable?

Individuals who organize junkets are known as *junket-masters*. They are responsible for compiling lists of *bonafide* gamblers and setting up their trips to Vegas. The sponsoring hotel-casino pays junket-masters for performing this service. Once you establish a reputation with one junket-master, don't be surprised if you hear from others. In big cities, the competition for good junket gamblers is fierce...and the high-limits player will often be deluged with invitations to junkets at several different casinos.

One final observation about getting on junkets. Some of you might want to receive casino comps, but don't want to go on organized junkets. Others of you might want to go on junkets but can't, because there are none leaving from your area. Do not despair. If you've got sufficient money to gamble and the casino likes your action, you can set up your own junket. What you are doing, in effect, is cutting out the middleman (junket-master), and dealing directly with the casino. You call the hotel and arrange your trip. Once the dates are established, you purchase your ticket and fly out. When you arrive at the sponsoring hotel, you present your bill for the trip at the casino cage, where you will be reimbursed for your flight. Then it's "drink, eat, and have a suite"...all on the house.

I used to set up my own junket when I was into the junket scene. It gave me more opportunity to be by myself and, most important, allowed me to visit and leave Vegas whenever I wanted. Being able to exit Las Vegas on the spur of the moment (not having to wait till the end of a regularly scheduled junket) can often mean the difference between winning and losing at the tables. This little drama is played out far too often: a member of an organized gambling junket makes a big killing his first day at the tables, only to lose all of it back while waiting for the end of his junket to leave.

Should You Go on a Junket?

By the time you finish reading this book, you will be able to answer the question for yourself. Some people say "If you're going to gamble big anyway, you might as well get the casino to pay your expenses." There is a lot of truth to that statement. But I also know others who warn that "casino comps make gamblers feel indebted to the house . . . and that affects their willingness to win at the tables."

What kind of gambler are you? Can you remain unseduced and guiltless in the face of casino favors? Can you keep your gambling in bounds when you're supposed to be a "high roller" and the casino is checking to make sure you're "in the action?" If you can, then maybe junkets are for you.

Want to know what I do? I seldom go on junkets anymore.

The Year 'Round Santa

Here's an incredible little item of interest: a few premium Vegas hotel-casinos give away so many freebies, they have to hire a special employee to distribute the goodies. The designation for this employee is, appropriately, casino host. His job? To draw high-rolling gamblers to his hotel and develop them into steady, loyal casino customers. "Actually, his job is to make them think they have died and gone to heaven."[10]

The casino host is an "ambassador of good will" . . . an individual who wants to make gamblers feel good about the hotel and casino where they might lose thousands, even hundreds of thousands, of dollars yearly. The host is something of a cross between a genie and Santa Claus, granting wishes and bearing gifts to those gamblers the casino favors.

And what gifts! One host gives his best customers gold money clips, each with a negotiable, black ($100) casino chip inside. Another makes sure that the wives of

33

valued gamblers are showered with gifts...everything from orchids and discounts at the hotel gift shops to rolls of coins for slot machine play. (These hosts are clever. They know that keeping the wives happy at the slots means the high-rolling husbands are left free to gamble for big stakes at the tables.)

The host uses his influence and Vegas savvy to arrange any activities gamblers desire. They might include getting front seats in a sold-out dinner show, arranging a round of golf, or setting up a tour to the Grand Canyon. Remember, the host is there to get the gambler what he wants. Period.

Some of the hosts are given the *"power of the pencil."* This is the ultimate authority in the giveaway sweepstakes, and only a few individuals in each hotel possess it. Those who do can use "the pencil" to authorize literally any kind of freebie...including a *totally* free stay in Las Vegas. A totally "comped" trip can easily run into thousands of dollars...so you can see how a host with "the pencil" might be a good person to have as a friend!

Why Is The Man With "The Pencil" So Nice?

Because he wants your business. And not just once...but time and time again. A loyal high roller is the biggest asset any casino can have. For that reason, each one is courted with all the pomp and enthusisam afforded a first-round draft choice for the NFL. The hope, of course, is that the personal bond established between host and player will be strong enough to tie the high roller to a specific casino, the one in which the host is employed.

The host is nice to the player for another reason: he

makes gambling losses easier to swallow and winnings more difficult to achieve. After all, if you have to lose, you might as well lose to people you like, right? And if you're going to win, you don't want to win money from people you like, right? "Cushion the losses and limit the wins": such should be the motto of your amiable casino hosts.

The Free Lunch As Last Meal

Here's a "free lunch" story to top them all. The manager of a well known Vegas showroom entertainer had a weakness when it came to freebies. He liked them. . .a lot. One day he was offered four roasted turkeys, on the house. He accepted, gladly. While he waited for the kitchen staff to wrap up his four birds, he wandered over to the crap tables. Suffice it to say he wasn't very lucky that day. His losses were such that, by the time he picked up his "free lunch," each turkey had cost him a cool $25,000![11]

* * *

There are, as we have seen, many different kinds of freebies in Vegas. But, whether they be free drinks at the tables, an all-expenses-paid junket, or a token of friendship from a casino host, all freebies serve the same function:

(1) to get you gambling and keep you gambling;
(2) to encourage poor gambling, in the form of:
    (a) showoff gambling;
    (b) gambling where you lose to "pay back" the freebies;
    (c) gambling where you hesitate to win big because you feel guilty taking money from the freebie-givers.

The dream merchants aren't philanthropists, and they certainly aren't dumb. When they "give away" money it's for a reason: to get more money in return. To the casino operators, "comps" are viewed as investments— as sensible ways to stimulate business and increase profits.

There is an old saying. You've all heard it. "There is no such thing as a free lunch." That's true in Vegas, too. For those of you who might want to partake of the free meal, be careful, or you might end up with your just desserts.

CHAPTER 5

IT'S ONLY MONEY

"When I go to Vegas I intend
to do some spending. I like to
cut loose every once in a
while. Besides, what the hell?
It's only money."
—*A Vegas Visitor*

Think back over your life. You'll notice that certain events stand out in your memory. My very first trip to Vegas produced such an event, and I remember it vividly to this day.

I had just entered the Desert Inn for my first go at casino gambling. I was nervous and excited...I really didn't know what to do or expect. I decided to make some bets in the $1.00-$5.00 range, and see how I would fare. Pulling out my wallet, I made my way to the cashier's window and handed over five $20 bills—my total gambling stake—to the lady behind the counter.

"Could I have some change, please," I asked.

The woman didn't blink an eyelash. "Sure," she replied, and handed me back a hundred dollar bill.

* * *

After my experience at the Desert Inn, I came to understand something basic and vital to the Nevada economy: *money doesn't mean much* and *money means everything* in Las Vegas. How can such a paradox be explained? This way: money means everything to those who *live* in Vegas, those who depend on it for survival; while money doesn't mean much to those who *visit* Vegas, those who spend it for a good time.

Furthermore, the *reason* why money doesn't mean much to the tourists is because they've been "psyched" into *thinking* it doesn't mean much. The whole Vegas environment has been created to support such a viewpoint. Put another way, the whole town has been designed to encourage free and plentiful spending by a willing and satisfied clientele. Take, for example:

Currency Devaluation—Vegas Style

One way to get people to spend more is make them think money is worth less. The dream merchants realize this and work hard to make dollars seem less valuable in Vegas. They accomplish this in several ways.

One way is to increase the price of everything in town. The result? As one gambling expert notes: in Vegas "...money quickly loses importance. Everything is overpriced and, in a remarkably short period of time, a ten dollar bill seems like a dime."[12]

Another way is to substitute money for chips in the

casinos. People tend to forget that the cute little red, green, or black disks in their hands are, in reality, $5.00, $25.00 and $100.00 bills. Such memory lapses can be very costly. To make matters worse, the dealers refer to the $5.00 and $25.00 chips as "nickel" and "quarter" chips, respectively. How's that for making money seem worthless!

Credit in Vegas accomplishes this same "currency devaluation" effect. Playing against a credit line can be devastating to your financial health when you consider that the gambler never sees any cash in any of his transactions. How easy it becomes to simply say, "I'll take a thousand more." No need to reach for your wallet and see what a thousand dollars really looks like. Simply sign the marker and place your bets. It's all so unreal...so much like playing monopoly. "Is this really money?" you start asking yourself. Believe me, it is.

The "currency devaluation" strategy is one way you're encouraged to spend money in Vegas. It is not the only strategy, nor is it the most powerful. The primary technique for keeping Vegas "green" involves creating in each visitor:

The Urge to Splurge

I have already discussed the Vegas "party atmosphere" in an earlier chapter, along with the notion of "socially justified indulgence." In Vegas, social standards are turned upside down: frugality is held up to ridicule while conspicuous consumption is praised. The town of Vegas has been designed to produce a "splurge" mentality in those who visit it...and within its magical borders the spendthrift replaces the skinflint as town hero.

Part of the splurge mentality is generated from the visitor's realization that in Vegas you can have almost anything for a price. "You mean I can buy *that* here?" is a common question heard throughout the city. Visitors are amazed that they can purchase anything from a prime seat at a sold-out dinner show to the company of a chorus girl who danced in the sold-out dinner show.

And do they buy! Dignified, upstanding citizens from Anywhere U.S.A., who wouldn't be caught dead paying their way into a line back home, gleefully "press the flesh" of the accommodating *maitre d'*, and then strut proudly to their "toked" showroom seats like bluebloods to their royal boxes. Once there, it's all they can do to keep their swelled heads from bursting.

After the show, these same individuals push into the casino, throwing caution to the wind. After all, when you've just bought your way into the royal box you don't bet silver dollars at the tables. Which brings us to another way the dream merchants encourage the separation between you and your money:

Feel Like a King, Spend Like a King

If Nevada were ever to mint a coin, its face should bear this inscription: "Every gambler a king." Because that's the way it is in Vegas. Where else can a person be treated like royalty—afforded front-row everything—simply because he is willing to gamble in a casino. Being treated regally is a great feeling, particularly Vegas-style, and "... millions of people will lose billions of dollars to taste it."[13]

Instant royalty. The dream merchants do everything they can to make a player feel special, for they know that once he feels like a king, he'll try to spend like one.

Which all means, if you gamble...be prepared to be pampered, spoiled, and generally treated in a manner befitting royalty.

Do not underestimate how "high" this treatment can make you feel...or how quickly it can make you want to throw your money around. Before I learned how to psych out Vegas, that's exactly how I used to react on my Vegas junkets. I'd arrive at my hotel...waiting for me would be a big basket of fruit and a personal note of welcome from the casino manager. Wherever I walked in the hotel, people knew me by name and treated me with the utmost courtesy and respect. At the gourmet restaurant, I always got the finest service and best food... always at my own special table. And when I went to gamble, the dealers always made room for me, letting everyone know that I was someone "special." Hell, all I needed was a crown and I figured I could have *owned* the hotel. Instead, I ended up investing in the place via my crap table losses. I had been "psyched" by the dream merchants. I wasn't a king after all...but I had been royally screwed.

Remember, the dream merchants enjoy making people think they are kings because it encourages them to splurge!... particularly at the tables where the greatest Vegas profits are realized. It is sad but true that, too often, the Vegas visitor is flattered by a touch of royal treatment, sticks his nose in the air, then ends up paying handsomely through it. But that won't be you...will it?

Money As Macho

Vegas is an interesting city. Even as our country teeters toward equal rights for women, Vegas remains overwhelmingly dedicated to the titillation of the male ego, a place where the average man can live out his cherished fantasies...for a price.

Why is Vegas a male town? Because the dream merchants cater to those who will enrich the city. And in Vegas, the major proportion of gambling revenue comes from males—either directly (through their own play), or indirectly (through the play of female companions—wives, girlfriends—brought along on the trip). Unless this picture changes radically—which it well might with the emergence of the "new woman"—Vegas will remain male in orientation: designed to satisfy male needs and encourage male spending.

The dream merchants understand the male ego well, and have designed their casinos to take full advantage of it. They know, for example, that many men bet higher and more impulsively in the presence of women because such men equate *money with macho*...these men believe that the more they can put on the tables, the more masculine they are. Tommy Renzoni, the man who brought baccarat to Vegas, pegged the male tendency perfectly, when he observed: "Women, it seems to me, have always made a positive difference at a gaming table...If a beautiful woman is actually playing at a Baccarat table, or in any other game for that matter, time and time again you'll see the activity at the table increase, the number of more substantial bettors grow."

The casino operators have not overlooked this connection between male wagering and female presence. "Every casino I've ever heard of," Renzoni notes, "will have good-looking female employees, shills, sitting at a gaming table playing with house money because they attract male players. They make the room more colorful, beautify it, but basically, they are there as a lure."[14]

The Sands Hotel, where Renzoni was employed for many years, practices what he preached. Whenever I gambled there, I was always impressed by the attractive shills sitting at the baccarat tables.

The casino's use of "female presence" does not end at the baccarat tables. In fact, the entire casino has a "sexual allure" to it . . . just the right kind of atmosphere to arouse the male macho and keep it at a swaggering pitch. Everywhere you look, scantily clad keno girls and cocktail waitresses are doing their parts to get men's blood pumping and money flowing. The casino decor adds to this sexual tapestry, with lots of sensual velvets and bordello reds. Even the games seem sexually oriented— particularly in craps where you can *make a pass, come, play the field,* and even get a *hard eight* (I'm modest, I don't bet the *hard ten*).

Before I developed my techniques for psyching out Vegas I fell prey to this "money as macho" temptation. I recall one incident in particular where my "macho" attitude cost me a bundle.

I had flown into Vegas with a young lady I really liked and dearly wanted to impress. We strolled into Caesars Palace and began playing craps. It was my turn to shoot. I put a $25 chip on the line and picked up the dice. Suddenly a guy appeared at the other side of the table and bet $50 on the *don't pass*. The hell with him, I thought, and I added $25 more to my bet. I lost on craps. The guy left his initial bet plus his winnings on the layout. I matched his bet with $100 on the pass line, and promptly crapped out again. $150 down the tubes. The guy let all his money ride. My god, a *desperado* . . . I muttered under my breath. My date looked at me, her warm brown eyes watching for me to exert my rightful superiority. I counted our quarter ($25) chips and stacked them neatly on *pass*. The guy across the table looked at me and smiled. I rattled the bones, wishing it was his throat in my hands.

"Craps, line away." The dealer vacuumed the layout with a sweep of his hand. Three craps...it couldn't happen! My adversary put four black chips ($400) on the *don't pass* line. What could I do? I reached for my wallet. Out came the hundreds. "Four hundred they *do*," I called out and placed four bills on the pass line. "Let's see a natural," I said, and threw the point number nine. Three rolls later I sevened out.

The guy across the table picked up his winnings and left, leaving me to ponder a stupid loss and a ruptured ego. Looking back on the whole silly episode, I now realize it could have been worse: my "adversary" could have *stayed* at the table while the dice remained cold. At which point I probably would have "steamed" my way into financial oblivion.

* * *

Casino owners get rich because they understand the link between a man's ego and his money. They know that when a player is losing (already a blow to his macho image), he'll sometimes use his credit line as a "salve" to ease his wounded pride; he'll ask for more money to "prove" his worth. It's almost as if he's saying, "See, I can get a thousand more...I'm worth plenty!" And the casino management is right there to grant his face-saving request.

In his novel, *Las Vegas Strip*, author Morris Renek captures the essence of this credit-line-for-macho strategy. He describes the plight of a gambler, a "Mr. Jackson," who is losing rapidly and signing markers for more chips. The casino boss, "Yank," grants Jackson's requests for money, each time saying "Mr. Jackson is good" for the funds. The effect is stunning:

" 'Mr. Jackson is good.' (Yank's) startling, old-fashioned call was not to be forgotten. The

heavier Jackson fell into debt, the deeper was the
need for Yank's protective voice. 'Mr. Jackson is
good.' Now it was needed like a drug, like fresh
air. The words were a simple credit rating, yet
they worked as well as any to bear witness that a
man was upright. . . . 'Mr. Jackson is good.' This
declaration upholding his name rolled on through
the night until the listeners were mesmerized. It
was easy to imagine how fine it would be if one
could hear this declaration about oneself.
'Mr. . . . . . is good.' It would be worth anything to
have this said with such authority to a roomful of
worldly people about your life on this earth."[15]

The Bottom Line

Money as macho. Just another way players can be
psyched out by the dream merchants. It is amazing
how many gamblers lose because of personal hangups,
NOT house percentages. These hangups can be overcome. . . I overcame them, so can anybody willing to ex-
pend the necessary effort.

If you want to beat Vegas you have to have the proper
mental attitude. Thinking "it's only money" is *not* a
proper mental attitude. Splurging and throwing your
money around isn't, either. Nor is using money to prove
your masculinity. *A proper mental attitude:* in order to
win money in Vegas, it's the bottom line.

CHAPTER 6

WHY IS THIS MAN SMILING?

> "The casino wins when the
> player loses. If you were a
> casino owner, would you
> rather see winners or losers at
> the tables?"
> —*Las Vegas Bell Captain*

"Show me a happy loser...and I'll show you a sucker." That's the opinion of many gambling authorities. Well, in Vegas that means there's a townful of suckers...because Vegas produces losers...and most of them *are* happy.

Why are losers smiling in Las Vegas? It is *not* because they are suckers...it is because they are *psyched* or *sick*...or a little bit of both. Let me elaborate.

The "Psych Factor"

How do you psych a gambler into feeling good about losing? Casino owners aren't fools. They understand that happy losers will return to Vegas to lose again. And repeat business keeps the Vegas lifeblood flowing.

Vegas is probably one of the only cities in the world that loves losers. "When you lose, everyone seems so sympathetic and understanding," explained one player to me recently. And why not? Every time the visitor loses, Vegas wins... and what business do you know of that doesn't treat its best customers well? One casino manager said it all, when he observed: "I never met a loser I didn't like."

The next time you visit Vegas, step into a casino and observe the happy loser "psychout" first hand. Look around for a gambler who is down to his last few chips, and see how he's treated. Observe the cocktail waitress bringing him a free drink to "make him feel better." Listen to the floorman commiserate with the hapless player, telling him he's never seen such a bad luck streak, and how things will surely change. Follow the player as he goes into the dinner show to be entertained by a comedian who makes him laugh and forget about his slaughtered bankroll. Watch as he leaves the showroom and wanders along the Strip, where the promise of a luckier tomorrow glitters through the neon-studded night.

Nick the Greek, probably the most famous gambler of our time, had an interesting philosophy about gambling. Profit and loss were important to the Greek, but they weren't the end-all of his profession. Even after he'd lost a great deal of money, he'd be quick to emphasize that "your life doesn't go with it." And that's the way Vegas wants the player to feel. "Hey," the town seems to be saying, "Sure you might lose, but your life doesn't go with it. So have fun, we love you, and maybe next time you'll beat the tables." Many gamblers seem to agree, losing with a smile on their faces, and these kinds of comments on their lips:

"I come to Vegas with a certain amount to lose. I figure the entertainment value of the gambling justifies the expenditure."

"If I wasn't spending money at the tables, I'd be spending it somewhere else. A night on the town or an evening at the casino—what's the difference?"

"So what if I lose some money? Look at all the fun I'm having in the meantime."

With such attitudes, it's hard to convince happy losers that they are, in fact, losers *period*. They've been psyched into accepting their financial depletion in a positive light. Nor are these attitudes likely to change when you consider how *winners* are treated in Vegas. You see, it's not nearly as much fun being a winner as a loser in Nevada: casino owners don't look fondly upon winners, and they let them know it in no uncertain terms.

Some people will argue that Vegas loves winners. This is simply not true. Casino owners love the *publicity* that winners generate . . . but don't let that fool you. The occasional winner is touted . . . but the steady winner is a target for scorn, and even expulsion from the casino. Don't take my word for it; ask any competent blackjack counter . . . if you can find one who hasn't been barred from casino play.

In a later chapter, I will be discussing this prejudice against winners in greater detail . . . telling you what you can do to protect yourself and keep winning. At this juncture, my purpose is to warn you about the negative treatment of winners and to emphasize that such treatment makes it psychologically more difficult to come out ahead. Most players don't enjoy being hassled or disliked—and believe me, you will be very hassled and greatly disliked if you are a steady winner in Las Vegas casinos.

The Sick Factor

Some players are psyched into losing. Others don't need to be psyched at all—they *want* to lose. To me, *these* are the people who should be barred from the casinos, before they can commit financial suicide.

If you spend any significant amount of time in casinos you will learn to spot these gambling lemmings who make their suicidal run at the tables. It is not a pretty sight...in fact, even the casino bosses tend to take a dim view of these sick players. The player who wants to lose is a liability for everyone: himself, his loved ones, even Vegas. His actions tend to give gambling a bad name...and the money he loses creates more ill will than it is worth.

It is surprising how many gamblers have some of this "desire to lose" tendency in them. Let me repeat: a person who wants to lose in Vegas has no business being there...anymore than a diabetic should be dallying around the local bakery. It would be well if all gamblers heeded the words of baccarat expert Tommy Renzoni:

"The next time you are about to enter a casino, ask yourself, 'Do I really *want* to win?' A silly question? Think about it. Many people gamble to lose because they lack self-esteem. Or because they want to atone for guilt. Or for a variety of psychological reasons. These are all an extra edge for the house... If you want to gamble, do it to win."[16]

The Psych Factor and/or The Sick Factor = Gambling Disaster

Above, you have a simple formula for defeat at the tables. Vegas has been designed to psych players into losing "with a smile." Unfortunately, sometimes this "psychout factor" can push a normal gambler into the realm of the sick gambler, with all its attendant risks and heartaches.

In the final chapter of this book I will have a personal message for those gamblers who walk the narrow line between being "psyched" and being "sick." It is vital that each of you accurately and honestly assess your own gambling behavior—you must decide for yourself whether you can control your play at the tables. If, after reading this book, you decide you cannot control your gambling ... then you will have to eliminate Las Vegas from your life. If you enjoy gambling as much as I do, then that kind of a decision will be one of the most difficult you will ever make. Yet, it is a decision which must be made if you are to ensure your financial survival and self-esteem. At one point in my life I was faced with just such a decision... and had I not been able to psychout the dream merchants and get my gambling under control, I would have been forced to leave Las Vegas—forever.

CHAPTER 7

GAINING THE MENTAL EDGE

"Many players . . . act like kids
in a candy factory when it
comes to gambling. It's truly
amazing the way some people
approach the gambling tables.
True, to many, it's an afford-
able form of enjoyment. But
I'll always believe that it's
more fun to win, whether the
game is bridge, gin rummy,
poker, craps, blackjack, or
roulette. You'll not only find
winning by design an enjoyable
experience but also something
that will give you an additional
measure of fulfillment, as well
as a greater appreciation of the
games you play."

—Len Miller, Editor
Gambling Times *Magazine*

How quickly would you lay down an even money bet if you knew the odds of winning were 3-1 against you? Probably not very quickly...if at all. Well, then, consider this: the way most people gamble, the odds are 3-1 against them the moment they enter a casino. First, they're battling the house percentages at the tables; second, they're combatting the casino tactics designated to psych them out; and third, they're fighting themselves.

Now, here's some good news: the odds don't have to be against *you*. You don't have to be the typical, psyched out gambler. You can change the odds—even tip them in your favor—if you can gain the psychological edge against the casinos and gamble in an intelligent, self-controlled fashion. This will involve what *Gambling Times* editor Len Miller calls *winning by design*. Consistent winning is not an accident, nor is it a matter of good luck. Frequent success at the tables is something that happens because you have planned and worked for it. Giving you a design for winning—for psyching out Vegas—is what this book is all about.

Self-Control: The Key to Winning

Whether you win or lose, your battle against the house will hinge, in large part, on your ability to maintain self-control in the face of casino countermeasures. Some gamblers have never even attempted to establish self-control in their play...others have made an effort, but it is either insufficient or forgotten in the heat of action. This is unfortunate, because more money is lost through the erosion or lack of self-discipline than any other factor.

Achieving effective self-control at the tables involves the willingness to learn and use the various techniques I will be presenting in the following chapters. Some of these techniques will be easy to master; others will require more time and effort.

When you first put these techniques into practice you might feel they are limiting your gambling spontaneity, and putting undue restrictions on your action. Don't despair—these feelings will pass. In fact, once you become proficient at gaining the mental edge, you will enjoy your gambling more than ever.

Learning how to achieve self-control in order to beat the casinos is like getting in good physical shape: at first it's an effort, even uncomfortable...but after a while you start feeling better, healthier...and it all seems well worth it. Get into the habit of self-control at the tables, and your efforts will pay off in handsome dividends, both financially and psychologically.

The Game Plan

To turn that 3-1 edge around and turn the odds in your favor, I have developed a game plan which will allow you to play effectively against the casino.

Understanding house percentages and how to play "smart" are aspects of effective gambling, and will be described in Chapter 8. Good sense makes good dollars, and part of good sense is playing the percentages. Good bets and sucker bets are indentified along with the best games to play, percentagewise, for the player. It is amazing how your self-esteem and control will increase when you begin to play "tough."

Money management is also crucial to winning at the tables—in fact, it might well be the major weapon at your disposal in psyching out Vegas. Principles of sound money management are presented in Chapter 9.

Did you realize that casinos can be—and have been—beaten? Chapter 10 describes a series of casino *coups* in blackjack, craps, roulette and baccarat. It's nice to know that Vegas can be cracked—that the player can win. Throughout the chapter, I have provided references so you can learn more about winning at the game(s) you choose to play.

One problem with winning is finding casinos that will allow you to continue to play. Chapter 11 tells you how you can win but not get barred from play.

This leads to a general discussion of "How To Choose And Use A Casino," the topic of Chapter 12. Contrary to popular opinion, not all casinos are the same— some give you a better shot at fattening your bankroll. And that's where you should be taking your business.

Regardless of where you gamble, playing in the right "frame of mind" is vital for that all-important, winning edge. In Chapter 13, I'll be showing you how to eliminate the *"psychological governors"* which restrict your gambling effectiveness and reduce your chances of winning at games of skill and chance.

Want to try your hand at poker? You'll find plenty of games in Vegas and, if you're not good, plenty of chances to lose your shirt. Playing poker in a casino is different from the Saturday night hometown game . . . so I recommend you study the poker guidelines presented in Chapter 14 before you bet a fistful of chips, then draw to an inside straight.

Chapter 15 offers a thumbnail summary of all the material presented in this book. The chapter is designed to serve as a handy reference for quick review before each gambling trip.

Chapter 16 provides a list of various non-gambling activities available in and around Las Vegas. I am hopeful that you will schedule some of these activities into your next gambling trip to create a more balanced itinerary, and to discourage excessive play at the tables.

Want to try your hand at gambling somewhere besides Las Vegas? Chapter 17 tells your what you can expect, particularly in the casinos of Lake Tahoe, Reno and Atlantic City.

Some people shouldn't be gambling—no matter where they travel nor how much they enjoy wagering. In "A Personal Note To The Degenerate Gambler" (Chapter 18), I address these individuals. If you are a degenerate gambler, think you might be, or aren't sure...please take time to read this section closely. If you don't think you've got a gambling problem, read the chapter anyway. It might help you avoid some tragic pitfalls in your gambling future.

In the final section of the book (Appendix A), I have provided an annotated bibliography so you can read further about gambling topics. I hope you will. Knowledge is a great weapon to wield in your battle against the casinos.

Let's Go

Enough of game plans and introductory comments. The tables are waiting... let's start turning them in your favor.

CHAPTER 8

LOOK MA, NO BRAINS

"Smart is better than lucky."
— "Titanic" Thompson

Let me ask you a question. Suppose you want to buy some stocks. One broker charges over 5% to handle your transaction, while another will do it for under 3%. Which broker would you use?

Here's a second question. Let's say you have money to risk, and you're considering two similar investments. One investment, however, could be made at half the risk of the other. Which investment would you choose?

Such simple questions, you say, with such obvious answers. So tell me, how do you explain this? In certain Nevada casinos you can play roulette on either an "American" or a "European" wheel. The house advantage on the American wheel is about double that of the European model (5.26% vs. 2.70%)...yet, the American wheels attract players...even when the "better deal"

European models are just a few steps away on the casino floor.

Playing an American wheel when a European model is available is equivalent to using the 5% broker, or choosing the investment that was double the risk.

Gambling authority Allan Wilson is puzzled by this seemingly senseless behavior. "It will forever be a mystery to (me) why roulette players did not *flock* to the clubs that first introduced the more generous (European) wheel. An even bigger mystery is how these clubs that sport *both* types of wheels can do any business on the two-zero (American) wheel."[17]

Mr. Wilson is being kind. In fact, there is no mystery to this behavior at all. The simple, sad truth is that, when it comes to gambling, many players check their brains at the casino door. I echo the sentiments of high-rolling gambler Lyle Stuart, when he observed: "It has always fascinated me that a person will spend years getting an education in order to acquire a skill that will pay off in good income and then will go to a gambling casino and waste much of that good income on games of which the person has almost zero knowledge."[18]

My own casino observations have convinced me that many casino gamblers are bent on attaining the lowest common denominator of human intelligence at the tables. Some players just don't know anything about the games . . . they blindly place their bets, hoping that some divine force will intercede in their behalf. Others seem to know what they're doing, but what they're doing is so stupid . . . which makes matters all the worse. Did these people spend their lives in some deep-space probe? Are they aliens visiting Earth, exploring a casino as our astronauts might examine some far-flung planetary structure? Certainly their betting behavior shows no earthly reasoning! In fact, their actions might be almost funny, if they weren't so pitiful. And costly.

Ignorance Isn't Bliss

Let me share with you just a few examples of "brainless" gambling I have had the misfortune of witnessing in Vegas. These are not isolated cases. If I told you of all the inept play I've observed, neither of us would ever finish this book!

* I was watching a player at the blackjack tables. He was dealt two aces. "I'm busted," he said, flipping his cards over for the dealer to see.

"What do you mean?" the dealer inquired, not knowing quite what to make of the situation.

"I got a twenty-two...isn't that a bust?"

The dealer was flabbergasted. So was I. I didn't wait around to see the rest of the carnage. (By the way, if you don't understand why this particular player was sitting on his brains, please don't play 21!)

* Another intellectual giant was perched at the rail of the crap table betting $5 chips on the BIG 6 and BIG 8. I asked him why he didn't *place* the 6 and 8, and get better odds at 7-6.

"What's a *place* bet?" the player wanted to know. I knew he'd have to find out in a hurry. With the extra house percentage he was paying by betting BIG 6 and BIG 8...he wouldn't be around for very long.

* Stopping off at the Sahara one afternoon, I spotted a man hovering over the roulette table, hunched like a praying mantis ready to strike. After numerous spins he finally put a $25 chip on red.

"When do you decide to bet?" I asked.

"After four blacks come up in a row."

I nodded. This man was playing the so-called "patience" system. You wait patiently until four blacks show and then bet red...figuring it's "due." Who knows, maybe the man had something there...maybe the little white ball remembered what happened those last four trips around the wheel. Maybe it was thinking to itself, "time for a black now, let's not screw up the law of averages." I'll say this: using the "patience" system, something probably will end up in the red...you.

* Another gambler was employing a different "system" at a roulette table across the casino. This time it was a lady, and she was betting the Martingale progression, chasing her money with a vengeance. I sidled up and asked how she was doing.

"I've won $50 already," she replied proudly.

"You're doubling up after a loss, right?"

"Yes, how did you know?" (It's amazing how many people think their "system" is a gambling secret known only to a few.)

"I played it myself once. You know," I added, "if you hit a run of bad luck it could wipe you out."

The lady looked at me like I was crazy. "My brother-in-law has been using this method for years...and it's paid for all his trips to Vegas."

What could I say? I hate in-laws who lie.

* I was downtown at Casino Center when I spotted a woman working two slot machines as fast as she could deposit her dimes. Suddenly she hit a jackpot. A shower of coins spilled into the payout-bowl, much to her delight. And she had a lot to be delighted about: the lighted figures on her progressive jackpot machine indicated a win of $534 dollars. Then, to my horror, she fed some more dimes into the machine and pulled the handle.

"My God," I shouted, rushing over. "Why did you do that?"

The woman spun around, startled by my outburst. "What's the matter?" she wanted to know, her graphite-black fingers tugging at the coins in her cup.

"You just erased your payoff!" I exclaimed.

The lady still didn't understand. "I got paid," she said, pointing to the pile of coins in the payout-bowl.

"The machine just pays part of it," I explained patiently. "Most of the $500 is paid by the change girl."

The woman's eyes opened real wide. "*What* $500?"

"The $500 you would have won...there...the figure on the top of the machine."

"I didn't know...." The woman's voice trailed off in a gasp. "I mean, nobody told me I won *that* money."

I wanted to tell her: "Well, if that doesn't take the jackpot!" But I didn't. Honest.

Gamble Smart...Or Don't Gamble At All

Would you like to know the really sad thing about the woman losing her jackpot? She's not an isolated case. Every year a king's ransom in jackpot dollars goes unpaid because players don't take the time to learn about the payouts on their machines.

In Vegas, the odds are tough enough to beat in the first place. To give the casino an extra edge through ignorance and/or stupidity is literally presenting it with a license to steal.

If you don't intend to gamble intelligently...take my

advice. Decide how much you can afford to lose at the tables, write that amount on a check, and mail it to your favorite casino. That way you can save the time and cost of going to Vegas. . . and still give yourself about the same chance of winning as if you had actually played in the casino.

Hiding the House Percentage: A Run Around the "Edge"

When it comes to winning at the tables. . . don't look to the casino owners for help. The woman at the slot machines found that out. . . the hard way. One must always remember that Vegas wins when the player loses, and the dream merchants aren't in business to cut their own throats. As a matter of fact, they *depend* on player ignorance to reap bigger profits—designing "psychout" ploys right into table games to take full advantage of player naivete.

The crap table provides ample evidence of this casino strategy. First of all, the best bet for the player isn't even inscribed on the layout! I'm referring to the "odds" bets, which can be made once a point number has been established. These bets pay off at true odds. . . which means that neither the casino nor the player has an advantage. The odds bet is the ONLY free wager in the casino. For that reason it isn't advertised, and *only* knowledgeable gamblers can take advantage of it.

When it comes to *bad* bets for the player, however, it's a layout of a different color. The wagers with the highest house percentages are very clearly marked on the table, and placed in a manner to encourage bets. The proposition bets—financial suicide to any gambler—are prominently positioned in the center of the layout where they can't be missed. The "field" also takes up a large amount of space, and it's located directly in front of the player to make wagering easy and tempting.

If, by chance, the player is blind or oblivious to the betting temptations before him on the green felt, the friendly stickman is always ready to recommend the bad bets. The intelligent player avoids such suggestions like the plague . . . but the gambler who doesn't understand the game is often taken in by such a "carney hustle." Don't blame the stickman for encouraging such poor play. It's his job to hustle for the house—to hawk bets that have a high casino advantage. If the player is dumb enough to get suckered in . . . well, whose fault is that? Gambling is a business and the player (customer) should remember the consumer credo: "Let the buyer beware."

If you want to be a winning gambler you must have a thorough knowledge of the games on which you bet. Casino owners get rich by exploiting player ignorance at the tables. Like, for instance, using the word "for" instead of "to" in designating payoffs on wagers. That little word change might not seem like much . . . but the difference in meaning can add up to whopping profits for the house. Consider, for example, the 12 number bet at roulette. When the house pays off at 2-*to*-1 odds, the casino advantage is slightly over 5%. At 2-*for*-1 odds, however, the house percentage soars to just under 37%!

Savvy players understand the difference between the "to" and "for" distinctions on the layout, and they frequent those establishments that give them the best odds at the tables. These same individuals are the ones who end up playing at casinos with the most liberal blackjack rules, European roulette wheels, and double odds on craps. Smart gamblers don't visit casinos randomly . . . they only play at those establishments which give them the best chance of winning (see the Casino Analysis sheet for blackjack, page 83, and "How to Choose and Use A Casino").

Knowledge is power in the world of casino gambling. Do yourself a favor: play *smart* and give yourself an edge against the house.

Your Best Bets In a Casino

If you thoroughly understand the gambling game(s) you play, then you already know your best bets in a casino. *They are those wagers that have the lowest house advantage.* Let me repeat:

Your best bets in a casino are those that
have the lowest house advantage.

Please don't forget this...it's crucially important to your financial health in Vegas. You cannot expect to be a winner if you consistently make bets that carry a high house percentage. The casino owners realize this, of course, and that is why they encourage such wagers at the tables.

One of the major factors in psyching out Vegas is learning how to make wagers that are most favorable to the player. This means establishing the necessary self-control to pass up those games, and bets, where the casino edge is too great.

Alright, what constitutes an acceptable house edge in making wagers? Certainly there is some disagreement here...not all gambling authorities are equally conservative. Let me give you my advice:

Never, never place a wager in a
gambling establishment where
the house advantage exceeds
1.5%.

If you follow my advice...and I hope you will...it means that certain casino games must be completely off limits for play. Why? Because any bet you make will have an hour advantage greater than 1.5% (usually *much* greater).

Four Casino Games Worth a Gamble

If you want to be a "tough" player—a winning play-er—you'll have to restrict your action to the proper bets in blackjack, craps, baccarat and roulette. By limiting your wagering to these four games, employing the proper playing strategies at the tables, and managing your money wisely (see next chapter), you'll have a gambling chance of winning. The data in Table 8-1 suggests the following playing strategy, *vis-a-vis* the games to play and the bets to make. Table 8-2 will tell you what the maximum and minimum betting limits are in the casinos, as well as the number of facilities for each game.

Roulette

If you heed my advice and don't place any bet where the house advantage is greater than 1.5%, then you'll have to pass up roulette as it is played in the United States. Most Nevada casinos still use the double-zero wheel with its horrendous 5.26% edge—a surefire bankroll destroyer. Those that offer the single-zero wheel do *not* include the *"en prison"* feature. Thus, the house edge of 2.70% is still too high for smart money play.

It is only in some European casinos (like those in Monte Carlo) where roulette becomes a viable gamble . . . and then only on the even money bets (e.g., red-black, odd-even) where the *"en prison"* feature applies and drops the house edge to an acceptable 1.35%.

TABLE 8-1

SUMMARY OF HOUSE ADVANTAGES FOR VARIOUS CASINO GAMES AND WAGERS

CASINO GAME/BET	HOUSE ADVANTAGE (IN %)	EXPECTED PLAYER LOSS PER $100 WAGERED *
Roulette:		
Double zero........................	5.26%	$5.26
Single zero........................	2.70%	$2.70
Single zero with *"en prison"* feature....	1.35%	$1.35
Craps: (Even money bets only)		
Pass/come bets.....................	1.414%	$1.41
Pass/come with single odds...........	0.848%	.85¢
Pass/come with double odds..........	0.606%	.61¢
Don't pass/don't come..............	1.403%	$1.40
Don't pass/don't come with single odds....	0.832%	.83¢
Don't pass/don't come with double odds..	0.591%	.59¢
Place bets: 6 and 8...................	1.51%	$1.51
All other bets on the layout have a house advantage between 2-17%.		
Baccarat:		
Bank (Includes 5% "commission').....	1.2%	$1.20
Player............................	1.3%	$1.30

Blackjack:

This is the only game where the player can gain the mathematical edge. This requires expert play, however. Otherwise, the house advantage can range between 2-10% (and even higher for poor play).

Slots:

The house advantage varies by machine and casino—usually it's around 20%. Some special $1.00 "carousel" machines have a 3-4% house edge.

Keno:

The house advantage averages about 20%

* Some of these figures are rounded off to the nearest whole number.

TABLE 8-2

LAS VEGAS BETTING LIMITS
MINIMUM AND MAXIMUM

CASINO	BLACKJACK # OF TABLES		MIN./MAX. ODDS	CRAPS # OF TABLES		MIN./MAX. ODDS	BACCARAT # OF TABLES		MIN./MAX	ROULETTE # OF WHEELS		MIN./MAX
DOWNTOWN LAS VEGAS												
California Club	23		1.⁰⁰ to $1000.⁰⁰	4	25 to $1000.⁰⁰		(D) 1-mini		2.⁰⁰ to $200.⁰⁰*	3		10¢ to $200.⁰⁰ max. payout
El Cortez	27		1.⁰⁰ to $500.⁰⁰	5	25¢ to $1000.⁰⁰		(D) 1-mini		2.⁰⁰ to $2000.⁰⁰	2		25¢ to $1000.⁰⁰ outside
Four Queens	40		1.⁰⁰ to $500.⁰⁰	5	1.⁰⁰ to $500.⁰⁰		(S) none			2		25¢ to $1000.⁰⁰ outside
Fremont	32		1.00 to $500.⁰⁰	6	25¢ to $500.⁰⁰		(S) 1-mini		2.⁰⁰ to $500.⁰⁰	3		10¢ to $500.⁰⁰ outside
Golden Gate	16		1.⁰⁰ to $200.⁰⁰	3	25¢ to $200.⁰⁰		(S) none			1		25¢ to $200.⁰⁰ outside
Golden Nugget	34		1.⁰⁰ to $500.⁰⁰	6	50¢ to $500.⁰⁰		(S) 1-mini		2.⁰⁰ to $500.⁰⁰	3		1.⁰⁰ to $500.⁰⁰ outside
Holiday International	22		1.⁰⁰ to $5.⁰⁰	3	25¢ to $500.⁰⁰		(S) none			1		10¢ to $200.⁰⁰ max. payout
Horseshoe	24		1.⁰⁰to $5000.⁰⁰**	6	25¢ to $5000.⁰⁰		(D) none			1		50¢ to $25,000.⁰⁰ outside
Hotel Nevada	7		1.⁰⁰ to $200.⁰⁰	1	1.⁰⁰ to $2.⁰⁰		(D) None			2		25¢ to $500.⁰⁰ outside
Lady Luck	16		2.⁰⁰ to $200.⁰⁰	3	2.⁰⁰ to $200.⁰⁰		(S) 1-mini		2.⁰⁰ to $200.⁰⁰	3		25¢ to $500.⁰⁰ outside
Las Vegas Club	22		1.⁰⁰ to $500.⁰⁰	4	50¢ to $500.⁰⁰		(D) none			1		25¢ to $200.⁰⁰ max. payout
Mint	62		1.⁰⁰ to $500.⁰⁰	4	1.⁰⁰ to $500.⁰⁰		(S) none			1		10¢ to $200.⁰⁰ max payout
Orbit Inn	9		50¢ to $50.⁰⁰	1	10¢ to $25.⁰⁰		(S)			4		1.⁰⁰ to $1000.⁰⁰ outside
Union Plaza	29		2.⁰⁰ to $500.⁰⁰	6	1.⁰⁰ to $500.⁰⁰		(D) 1-mini		2.⁰⁰ to $1000.⁰⁰			
Western Hotel	4		1.⁰⁰ to $50.⁰⁰	none			none			1		30¢ to $200.⁰⁰ max. payout
BOULDER HIGHWAY LAS VEGAS												
Nevada Palace	12		1.⁰⁰ to $200.⁰⁰	2	25¢ to $200.⁰⁰		(S) none			1		50¢ to $200.⁰⁰ outside
Sam's Town	26		1.⁰⁰ to $1000.⁰⁰	4	25¢ to $1000.⁰⁰		(D) 1-mini		2.⁰⁰ to $500.⁰⁰	3		50¢ to $1000.⁰⁰ outside
Showboat	24		1.⁰⁰ to $200.⁰⁰	2	1.⁰⁰ to $400.⁰⁰		(S) none			1		25¢ to $350.⁰⁰ max. payout

LAS VEGAS STRIP

Casino								
Aladdin	36	2.⁰⁰ to $1000.⁰	9	2.⁰⁰ to $1000.⁰⁰	(D) 2	20.⁰⁰ to $4000.⁰⁰	3	50¢ to $1000.⁰⁰ outside
Ambassador	6	2.⁰⁰ to $100.⁰⁰	1	1.⁰⁰ to $50.⁰⁰	(S) none		none	
Barbary Coast	26	2.⁰⁰ to $500.⁰⁰	6	1.⁰⁰ to $1000.⁰⁰	(D) 2-mini	5.⁰⁰ to $2000.⁰⁰	2	50¢ to $1000.⁰⁰ max. payout
Bingo Palace	21	1.⁰⁰ to $200.⁰⁰	2	1.⁰⁰ to $200.⁰⁰	(D) none		1	10¢ to $200.⁰⁰ max. payout
Caesars Palace	52	3.⁰⁰ to $3000.⁰⁰	11	3.⁰⁰ to $2000.⁰⁰	(S) 4	20.⁰⁰ to $8000.⁰⁰	8	2.⁰⁰ to $2000.⁰⁰ outside
Castaways	14	1.⁰⁰ to $500.⁰⁰	2	1.⁰⁰ to $500.⁰⁰	(D) none		1	25¢ to $25.⁰⁰ straight up
Desert Inn	30	2.⁰⁰ to $1000.⁰⁰	6	2.⁰⁰ to $1000.⁰⁰	(S) 3	20.⁰⁰ to $4000.⁰⁰	3	2.⁰⁰ to $1000.⁰⁰ outside
Dunes	35	2.⁰⁰ to $1000.⁰⁰	8	2.⁰⁰ to $2000.⁰⁰	(S) 4	20.⁰⁰ to 2000.⁰⁰	5	50¢ to $100.⁰⁰ straight up
Flamingo Hilton	40	2.⁰⁰ to $500.⁰⁰	6	1.⁰⁰ to $500.⁰⁰	(S) none		4	25¢ to $500.⁰⁰ outside
Four Kings	4	1.⁰⁰ to $25.⁰⁰	none		none		none	
Foxy's Firehouse	5	2.⁰⁰ to $50.⁰⁰	1	50¢ to $50.⁰⁰	(S) none		none	
Frontier**	21	2.⁰⁰ to $2000.⁰⁰	6	2.⁰⁰ to $1000.⁰⁰	(S) 1	25.⁰⁰ to $2000.⁰⁰	2	50¢ to $1000.⁰⁰ outside
Hacienda	19	2.⁰⁰ to $500.⁰⁰	3	2.⁰⁰ to $200.⁰⁰	(S) none		2	25¢ to $350.⁰⁰ max. payout
Holiday Inn	30	1.⁰⁰ to $500.⁰⁰	4	1.⁰⁰ to $500.⁰⁰	(D) none		2	1.⁰⁰ to $250.⁰⁰ outside
Imperial Palace	38	2.⁰⁰ to $500.⁰⁰	4	1.⁰⁰ to $500.⁰⁰	(S)	5.⁰⁰ to $2000.⁰⁰	2	25¢ to $500.⁰⁰ outside
King Eight	8	1.⁰⁰ to $200.⁰⁰	1	1.⁰⁰ to $200.⁰⁰	(S) none		none	
Landmark	18	1.⁰⁰ to $500.⁰⁰	3	$1.⁰⁰ to $500.⁰⁰	(S) none		2	1.⁰⁰ to $500.⁰⁰ outside
Las Vegas Hilton	32	2.⁰⁰ to $1000.⁰⁰	9	1.⁰⁰ to $1000.⁰⁰	(S) 3	5.⁰⁰ to $2000.⁰⁰	4	1.⁰⁰ to $1000.⁰⁰ outside
Little Caesar's	4	50¢ to $100.⁰⁰	1	50¢ to $100.⁰⁰	(S) none		none	
Marina	20	2.⁰⁰ to $500.⁰⁰	4	2.⁰⁰ to $500.⁰⁰	(S) none		2	1.⁰⁰ to $500.⁰⁰ outside
Maxim	24	2.⁰⁰ to $500.⁰⁰	3	2.⁰⁰ to $500.⁰⁰	(D) 1-mini	2.⁰⁰ to $500.⁰⁰	2	25¢ to $500.⁰⁰ outside
MGM Grand	70	2.⁰⁰ to $1000.⁰⁰	10	2.⁰⁰ to $1000.⁰⁰	(S) 3	20.⁰⁰ to $2000.⁰⁰	6	2.⁰⁰ to $50.⁰⁰ straight up
Mickeys Casino	2	50¢ to $10.⁰⁰	none		none		none	
Nob Hill	8	1.⁰⁰ to $200.⁰⁰	1	25¢ to $200.⁰⁰	(D) none		none	
Riviera	32	2.⁰⁰ to $1000.⁰⁰	6	2.⁰⁰ to $1000.⁰⁰	(S) 2	20.⁰⁰ to $4000.⁰⁰	2	1.⁰⁰ to $50.⁰⁰ inside
Royal Casino	9	1.⁰⁰ to $100.⁰⁰	2	1.⁰⁰ to $100.⁰⁰	(D) none		1	1.⁰⁰ to $25.⁰⁰ inside
Sands	22	2.⁰⁰ to $1000.⁰⁰	6	2.⁰⁰ to $1000.⁰⁰	(S) 2	20.⁰⁰ to $4000.⁰⁰	2	2.⁰⁰ to $1000.⁰⁰ outside
Shenandoah	20	2.⁰⁰ to $500.⁰⁰	3	2.⁰⁰ to $500.⁰⁰	(D) none		1	2.⁰⁰ to $500.⁰⁰ outside
Silver Bird	36	2.⁰⁰ to $1000.⁰⁰	5	2.⁰⁰ to $1000.⁰⁰	(S) none		2	2.⁰⁰ to $1000.⁰⁰ outside
Silver City	18	50¢ to $200.⁰⁰	2	50¢ to $200.⁰⁰	(S) none		2	10¢ $350.⁰⁰ max. payout
Silver Nugget	14	1.⁰⁰ to $100.⁰⁰	1	25¢ to $200.⁰⁰	(S) none		1	50¢ to $500.⁰⁰ outside
Silver Slipper	16	1.⁰⁰ to $500.⁰⁰	2	1.⁰⁰ to $500.⁰⁰	(D) none		1	25¢ to $25.⁰⁰ inside
Stardust	48	2.⁰⁰ to $1000.⁰⁰	7	2.⁰⁰ to $2000.⁰⁰	(S) 1; 1-mini 12.⁰⁰ to 2000 ‡		4	1.⁰⁰ to $1000.⁰⁰ outside
Treasury	17	2.⁰⁰ to $500.⁰⁰	2	2.⁰⁰ to $500.⁰⁰	(D) none		1	25¢ to $500.⁰⁰ outside
Tropicana	35	2.⁰⁰ to $1000.⁰⁰	6	2.⁰⁰ to $1000.⁰⁰	(S) 2	25.⁰⁰ to $8000.⁰⁰	2	2.⁰⁰ to $1000.⁰⁰ outside
Vegas World***	16	2.⁰⁰ to $1500.⁰⁰	1	2.⁰⁰ to $1000.⁰⁰	(S) none		1	⁺.⁰⁰ to $200.⁰⁰ outside

* (S) is single odds, and (D) is double odds on craps . . .
** The Frontier has the highest single deck limit in Las Vegas for blackjack
*** Vegas World is the only casino in Las Vegas to offer triple odds
‡ $4,000.⁰⁰ limit when initial bet is $500.⁰⁰

Recently, Atlantic City casinos have introduced a new wrinkle in roulette payoffs on the double zero wheel. Should the ball drop in 0 or 00, the gambler loses only half of the money he has wagered on the *even money* bets. This cuts the house percentage to a little more than 2½%—still unacceptable by my standards. All other bets on the Atlantic City roulette layout retain the 5.26% house edge. (The one exception to this 5.26% edge is the 5-number "line bet," which gives the house an even greater percentage.)

Roulette Playing Strategy

To maximize your chances for winning at roulette, always observe these three rules:

(1) Make even-money (e.g., red-black, odd-even) wagers ONLY.

(2) Play ONLY at those casinos that have single-zero wheels and permit the *"en prison"* feature.

(3) Utilize proper money management procedures while playing (see next chapter).

Craps

With the exception of EXPERT play at blackjack, craps affords the player the best gamble for his money. When the game is played with single or double odds, *there are no lower house percentage bets in the casino.* In fact, if all players wagered at craps intelligently, the house profits would be so low that the game would probably have to be changed to increase casino revenues. Fortunately—from the casino owners' viewpoints—such alterations won't be necessary as long as gamblers continue to ignore the low percentage odds-bets in favor of the proposition wagers, with their outrageous house advantage. Please, don't you gamble that way!

There is only one correct way to play craps, and that is to whittle the house percentage to a minimum. That means your bets should be restricted to either *pass* or *don't pass, come* or *don't come*, and the maximum odds bets allowed. As you will note in Table 8-1, casinos that offer double odds give the player a lower house advantage than those that offer only single odds. Therefore, you should restrict your play to those establishments that allow double odds wagers.

Remember, always take or lay the odds with your *pass, don't pass, come,* and *don't come* bets. *If you can't afford to wager the maximum allowable odds, then your line bet is too high.* The odds bets will help you cut the house percentage to rock bottom. Take advantage of them!

You will note that I also include the 6 and 8 place bets in Table 8-1. Although these bets aren't as good as the *line-come-odds* wagers, they still have a relatively low house advantage—just a fraction over the 1.5% allowable level. Thus, for those of you who *must* cover some number to be happy (and aren't satisfied doing so via the *come* bet to the box numbers), *place* the 6 and 8, and you'll still be playing "tough."

If you stick to the bets I have listed in Table 1 you will be playing craps as well as any so-called "professional." A person becomes a smart money gambler when he steadfastly refuses to make any other kind of bets at the crap tables. It takes self-control to stay away from those tempting, high-casino-advantage wagers . . . but you must if you want a chance to win at dice.

Craps Playing Strategy

In casino craps you can wager with or against the shooter. If you have the temperament and the desire to bet *don't pass* . . . go ahead; it is an excellent low-percentage wager (a fraction better than going with the dice). The playing strategy below, however, is based on betting WITH the shooter . . . because that is the way most dice players gamble at a crap table.

(1) *Pass line, come* and *odds* wagers are your best percentage bets at dice. Make NO other wagers at the crap table (except placing the 6 and/or 8, if you must have place bet action).

(2) Always wager the maximum odds allowable by the casino. Whenever possible play in establishments that permit double-odds behind the line. In casinos that allow single-odds only, wager three units on the pass line (if your bankroll is sufficient), so you can get better odds behind the line. (In most gaming establishments, when you have a three unit pass line bet, you can take three units behind the line on the point numbers 4 and 10; four units on the point numbers 5 and 9; and five units on the point numbers 6 and 8.)

(3) For the average player, betting the pass line and taking full odds will provide sufficient entertainment. If you are a player, however, who desires more action . . . then take one or two *come* bets after the point has been established, BUT NO MORE. If the dice are passing, taking *come* bets will help you win bigger, faster. If the dice are cold, however, *come* bets can make a shambles of your bankroll in a matter of minutes.

(4) Utilize proper money management procedures while playing craps (see next chapter).

Baccarat

This is another casino game with a house edge low enough to make it playable. In fact, the casino advantage at the baccarat "bank" and "player" wagers is lower than for the *pass* and *don't pass* bets at the crap tables. It is only when the gambler "takes the odds" that craps surpasses baccarat as the lower house-advantage game in Vegas.

Baccarat is probably the simplest casino game to play. It is a mindless game, made glamourous by the high stakes betting limits and plush playing area. Play of the hand is strictly regulated, and the gambler has no options except how much money he chooses to wager, and whether it will be on bank or player. In reality, baccarat is basically a trumped-up, coin-flipping exercise. You choose heads (banker) or tails (player), flip a few cards, and either win or lose.

To those of you who want to try your hand at baccarat, don't be afraid. As I said before, the game is played according to a fixed set of rules...you cannot make a mistake...and the dealers will be more than happy to assist you at the tables.

The only problem with baccarat for most Vegas visitors is the table limits. Baccarat is a high-stakes game, with the betting limits normally ranging from a $20 minimum up to $2,000, and even higher. That means that the game is pretty well off-limits to the hundred-dollar-a-day gambler. There are, however, some casinos that allow lower minimum bets...particularly on the mini-baccarat layouts that are springing up around town. If you want to play baccarat on a small budget you'll be able to do so...but you might have to shop around to find a low limit game (and when you do, it might not be as plush as the ones you saw in the premium Strip establishments).

One final note on baccarat. My discussion of the game is based on the "American" version...the version that is played in all U.S. casinos. There is, however, a European game of baccarat that is *very* different from the kind you'll encounter in Vegas. Do *NOT* play that game without a full understanding of the rules and percentages involved.

BACCARAT RULES
10's and Picture Cards Have No Value

IF PLAYER'S FIRST 2 CARDS TOTAL:	PLAYER (Wait for dealer's instructions before drawing)
0,1,2,3,4,5	Draws a card.
6,7	Stands.
8,9	Natural, Banker cannot draw.

BANKER

IF BANKER'S FIRST 2 CARDS TOTAL	DRAWS CARD WHEN PLAYER'S THIRD CARD IS:	DOES NOT DRAW WHEN PLAYER'S THIRD CARD IS:
3	1,2,3,4,5,6,7,9,10	8
4	2,3,4,5,6,7	1,8,9,10
5	4,5,6,7	1,2,3,8,9,10
6	6,7	1,2,3,4,5,8,9,10
7	Stands	
8,9	Natural. Player must stand.	

CASINOS	BACCARAT TABLES	LIMITS	MINI-B TABLES	LIMITS
ALADDIN	2	$20–$4000	0	—
BARBARY COAST	0	—	2	$5–$2000
CAESARS PALACE	4	$20–$8000	0	—
CALIFORNIA CLUB	0	—	1	$1–$200
DESERT INN	3	$20–$4000	0	—
DUNES	4	$20–$2000*	0	—
EL CORTEZ	0	—	1	$2–$500
FREMONT	0	—	1	$2–$500
FRONTIER	1	$25–$2000	0	—
GOLDEN NUGGET	0	—	1	$2–$500
HILTON	3	$5–$2000	0	—
IMPERIAL PALACE	2	$5–$2000	0	—
MAXIM	0	—	1	$2–$500
M-G-M	3	$20–$2000	0	—
MINT	0	—	1	$2–$200
RIVIERA	2	$20–$4000	0	—
SAHARA	2	$20–$2000	2	$2–$500
SAM'S TOWN	0	—	1	$2–$500
SANDS	2	$20–$4000	0	—
STARDUST	1	$5–$2000*	1	$2–$500
TROPICANA	2	$25–$8000	0	—
UNION PLAZA	1	$5–$1000	1	$2–$500
TOTALS	**32**	—	**13**	—

* Limit is $4000 when initial bet is $500.

Baccarat Playing Strategy

To maximize your chances for winning at baccarat, always observe these rules:
(1)   Make PLAYER or BANKER bets ONLY. Stay away from the proposition bets.
(2)   Baccarat is a big-money game. Don't get in over your head . . . and don't let the elegant surroundings psych you into spending more than you can afford to lose.
(3)   Utilize proper money management procedures while playing (see next chapter).

Blackjack

More books and articles have been written about this casino game than any other . . . and for good reason. Blackjack can be beaten. It is the *only* casino game where the gambler can gain the mathematical edge, and consistently beat the house. To do so, however, requires skillful play, proper money management, and a healthy dose of self-control. In fact, the "psyching" factor becomes critical in winning blackjack because: (1) the player must totally avoid emotional betting (e.g., hunches, steaming) and wager according to a pre-determined strategy; (2) the player must "psych" the casino personnel, camouflaging his actions so they won't think he's a counter, and bar him from playing (see Chapter 11).
If you are willing to take the time necessary to learn proper blackjack play . . . and if you have the temperament and self-control to adhere to that proper play *in the casino*, then "21" should be your game. In fact, you could make a living at playing blackjack, because the odds will be in your favor when you play the best game offered in Vegas.

cards...if he can be psyched out he's gonna
end up a loser. In this town they figure you'll
lose your shirt once you lose your head."

Don't you lose your head and maybe...just maybe... you'll have the casino by the tail!

Blackjack Playing Strategy

Providing a thorough blackjack playing strategy is far
more difficult than showing a player how to bet roulette
or shoot craps. This is because competent "21" play requires an in-depth knowledge of the game and the odds
which change with each turn of a card. Keeping in mind
all the variables regarding blackjack, there is a responsible way to play, generally referred to as Basic Strategy.
The Basic Strategy player can break even with the house
(and actually achieve a 0.15% edge at Caesars because of
their special rules).

Before laying down any money at 21, be sure to con-
sult Tables 8-3 through 8-5 on the following pages. Basic
Strategy is a way of playing without counting the cards
that offers the player the best winning edge. The hands
are played according to data compiled from exhaustive
computer runs which produced information on the hands
most likely to win. All responsible blackjack books offer
similar strategies. You will notice that Basic Strategy
varies according to the number of decks in play, as well
as to the location where blackjack is played. Keep in
mind, though, that Basic Strategy arms you with only a
little knowledge—enough to keep you playing and breaking even. (Basic Strategy is just the first step if you
want to learn to win.)

The following charts were developed by blackjack
"millionaire" Stanley Roberts:

TABLE 8-3

BASIC STRATEGY FOR SINGLE DECK PLAY

HARD HANDS

Player's Hand (hard totals)	Dealer's "Upcard"	Decision
12	2	H
12	3-6	S
13, 14, 15, 16	2-6	S
12, 13, 14, 15, 16	7, 8, 9, 10, Ace	H
17 or more	Any "upcard"	S

SOFT HANDS

Doubling On Soft Hands

Player's Hand	Dealer's "Upcard"	Decision
A2, A3, A4, A5	4,5,6	D
A6	2-6	D
A7	3-6	D
A8	6	D

Standing

When standing on soft hands use the following rules:

Player's Hand	Dealer's "Upcard"	Decision
A7	2-8	S
A8, A9	9, 10, A	S
A2, A3, A4, A5, A6	Any Upcard	H

Splitting Pairs

Always split 8's and Aces, and never split, 4's, 5's
and 10's. The chart shows splits on other pairs.

Player's Hand	Dealer's "Upcard"	Decision
2's	3-7	Split
3's	4-7	Split
6's	2-6	Split
7's	2-8	Split
9's	2-6, 8,9	Split

Doubling Down Strategy

Player's Hand	Dealer's "Upcard"	Decision
8	6	D
9	2-6	D
10	2-9	D
11	Any "upcard"	D

As can be seen, we never double down with hands
less than a hard eight, except for the soft hands.

TABLE 8-4

HARD STANDING STRATEGY:

Stand on...	...when the dealer's up-card is
13 or more	2, 3
12 or more	4, 5, 6
17 or more	7, 8, 9, 10, A

SOFT STANDING STRATEGY:

Stand on...	...when the dealer's up-card is
soft 18 or more	2, 3, 4, 5, 6, 7, 8
soft 19 or more	9, 10, A

You should hit any soft total less than 18 whatever the dealer's up card is.

HARD DOUBLING STRATEGY:

Double down on...	...when the dealer's up-card is
11	2, 3, 4, 5, 6, 7, 8, 9, 10
10	2, 3, 4, 5, 6, 7, 8, 9
9	3, 4, 5, 6

Never double down on a hard total of eight or less or on a hard total of twelve or more.

SOFT DOUBLING STRATEGY:

Double down on...	...when the dealer's up-card is
A,7	3, 4, 5, 6
A,6	3, 4, 5, 6
A,5 and A,4	4, 5, 6

With a soft total of nineteen or more, you should never double down but instead follow basic strategy for soft standing.

PAIR SPLITTING STRATEGY:

Never split 4,4.   Always split A,A.
Never split 5,5.   Always split 8,8.
Never split 10,10

Split the following pairs..	...when the dealer's up-card is
9, 9	2, 3, 4, 5, 6, *, 8, 9
7, 7	2, 3, 4, 5, 6, 7
6, 6	3, 4, 5, 6
3, 3	4, 5, 6, 7
2, 2	4, 5, 6, 7

* Note that you do not split 9's when the dealer's up-card is a 7.
NEVER TAKE INSURANCE

TABLE 8-5

Player's Hand	H = Hit S = Stand D = Double	SU = Surrender SP = Split						Dealer's Up-Card	
	2	3	4	5	6	7	8	9	10	A
A,A	SP	SP	SP	SP	SP	SP	SP	SP	SP	SP
2,2	SP	SP	SP	SP	SP	SP	H	H	H	H
3,3	SP	SP	SP	SP	SP	SP	H	H	H	SU
4,4	H	H	H	SP	SP	H	H	H	H	H
5,5				Play as a Hard Ten						
6,6	SP	SP	SP	SP	SP	H	H	H	H	SU*
7,7	SP	SP	SP	SP	SP	SP	H	H	SU*	SU*
8,8	SP	SP	SP	SP	SP	SP	SP	SP	SU*	SU*
9,9	SP	SP	SP	SP	SP	S	SP	SP	S	S
10, 10	S	S	S	S	S	S	S	S	S	S
A,2 & A,3	H	H	H	D	D	H	H	H	H	H
A,4 & A,5	H	H	D	D	D	H	H	H	H	H
A, 6	H	D	D	D	D	H	H	H	H	H
A, 7	S	D	D	D	D	S	S	H	H	H
A,8 & A,9	S	S	S	S	S	S	S	S	S	S
5, 6, 7	H	H	H	H	H	H	H	H	H	SU*
8	H	H	H	H	H	H	H	H	H	H
9	H	D	D	D	D	H	H	H	H	H
10	D	D	D	D	D	D	D	D	H	H
11	D	D	D	D	D	D	D	D	D	H
12	H	H	S	S	S	H	H	H	H	SU*
13	S	S	S	S	S	H	H	H	H	SU*
14 & 15	S	S	S	S	S	H	H	H	SU*	SU*
16	S	S	S	S	S	H	H	SU*	SU*	SU*
17	S	S	S	S	S	S	S	S	S	SU*

Never Take Insurance
* If Surrender is cancelled—Hit until Hard 17

TABLE 8-6
The Best and Worst Games in Las Vegas

BEST GAMES	NO. DECKS	RULES	PLAYER EDGE
Caesars Palace	1	DS: Sur.*	+.15%
Circus Circus Sahara Castaways Stardust Silver Slipper	1	Standard Strip	.00%
El Cortez	1	DS: Sur. Hit Soft 17	−.05%
Fremont	1	Sur.; Hit Soft 17	−.18%
Horseshoe; Mint	1	Hit Soft 17	−.20%
Riviera	2	Sur.	−.28%
Caesars Palace	4	DS; Sur.	−.31%
Flamingo Hilton	2	Standard Strip	−.35%
MGM	4	DS	−.38%
Las Vegas Club #	6	DS; Sur.; Hit Soft 17; Double on 3+ cards	−.40%
4 Queens	2	DS; Hit Soft 17	−.42%
WORST GAMES			
Golden Nugget Union Plaza	5	Hit Soft 17	−.76%
Mint	4	Hit Soft 17	−.71%
Frontier	6	Standard Strip	−.60%

*DS = **Double-down on split pairs.** Sur. = **Conventional Surrender.** # **Erroneously advertised as "The best blackjack rules in the world."**

(Remember, the information here is current as of this writing, but you should be aware of changing rules and circumstances.) When you play right, in the right place, you are put in the same winning position as the casino when it has the advantage.

TABLE 8-7

CASINO ANALYSIS SHEET

It would not be possible for us to give you an accurate analysis of where to play as the rules are constantly being changed (the casino lists are intended as a *guide*, though they were carefully researched and should be fairly reliable). At the moment, Las Vegas is favored, in general, over Tahoe, Reno or Atlantic City, due to its more liberal rules. We have, instead, presented a format for you to use in making your own analysis, when you arrive at the general area in which you will be playing. Take a piece of ruled paper (you may need more than one sheet) and place the headings down the side as indicated below:

The Casino Analysis Sheet is used as follows. On the left side are the rules or other conditions that will effect your overall percentage, followed by a number which is weighed in accordance to the effect that that rule or condition does affect your percentage. After checking out a casino, write the name of the casino on top and put in all the numbers that apply to that casino. The total is used to compare one casino to another, the higher the total, the better for the player. A Las Vegas Strip single deck game, no surrender or DASA, with a 39 card shuffle point would have a total of 466. A Reno single deck game with a 39 card shuffle point would have a total of 391. In general, try to play in a casino with a rating of at least 300.

Rule or Condition Points

Rule or Condition	Points	
INSURANCE	+210	
PAIR SPLITTING ALLOWED	+46	
RESPLITTING OF PAIRS EXCEPT ACES	+10	
RESPLITTING ALLOWED ON ACES	+10	
11	+89	
10	+56	
9	+14	
8	+1	
SOFT	+40	
LATE SURRENDER	+20	
EARLY SURRENDER	+65	
DOUBLING ALLOWED ON THREE OR MORE CARDS	+20	
DOUBLE AFTER SPLIT ALLOWED	+20	
if less than ½	do not play	
1/2	−100	
2/3	−25	
3/4	±0	
7/8	+25	
ALL	+100	
1	0	
2	−35	
4	−51	
5	−54	
6	−56	
MORE THAN 6	−65	
DEALER HITS SOFT 17	−20	
BLACKJACK PAYS EVEN MONEY	−206	
BLACKJACK PAYS DOUBLE	+206	
TOTAL		
NUMBER OF TABLES		

The best way to learn good winning strategy is by actually playing the game under the guidance of a skilled mentor (for example, taking lessons at the Stanley Roberts School of Winning Blackjack). Yet, some basic playing procedures can be presented here. For a more complete presentation of blackjack playing strategy, please refer to the recommended books discussed in Appendix A.

(1)   A highly knowledgeable friend of mine tells me there is only one favorable blackjack game in the state of Nevada—and that game can be found at the Nevada Club in Reno. It's a single deck game where all the cards are used (interestingly enough, the Nevada Club also has a single-zero roulette wheel). Other clubs use two or four deck shoes, with the game becoming less "player-favorable" as the number of decks increases.

(2)   Should you ever come across a game where the dealer wins all ties—forget it. If you play in such a game, you are giving the house a mammoth 9% advantage.

(3)   Tipping (toking) the dealer is part of every professional blackjack player's winning strategy—and it should be part of yours. Regular toking can not only make the game more friendly, it might cause the dealer to respond with little "signals" (both conscious and unconscious) that could work for you.

(4)   No matter how much you're winning, learn to act like a typical Las Vegas loser.

(5)   If a dealer shuffles arbitrarily or too often, he could be deliberately trying to hurt the player. Don't let him psych you into losing—there are plenty of tables—plenty of casinos you can play. When a dealer shuffles after you make a big bet, it's your

signal to shuffle off.

(6) A player who has mastered the basic rules of black-jack has options that are not available to the dealer: *splitting, doubling down, taking insurance, surrendering.* Once you master the basic rules, you are ready to learn Basic Strategy, methods for hitting, standing, doubling down, or splitting a pair (based on mathematical probability, as is shown in Tables 3 through 5, pages 77-81), and then. . .

(7) You should be ready for card counting because blackjack becomes more favorable for players who count. To get the winning edge you should become a card counter. There are card counting systems that range from simple to professional level (for the easiest-to-use, most effective count, see *Winning Blackjack* by Stanley Roberts, described in Chapter 19).

(8) You're safer playing in a major casino—avoid the small, out-of-the-way places, bars or private games. Select your casino carefully. You will generally be safer in the larger establishments. Your casino analysis sheet (p. 84) can help you keep a running tab on the changing rules and conditions of the individual blackjack games around town (for analysis of casinos in general, see Appendix A).

(9) A few miscellaneous tips:
—Always play at a well-lighted table.
—Try to avoid tables that are close to sources of loud noise (although you will never really find a quiet area in a major casino).
—If you can distinctly hear the cards being dealt, then that is a sufficiently low level of noise.
—Use good money management (see next chapter).

Casino Games To Stay Away From!

If you want to be a "tough" player you'll want to pass up those games and/or wagers where the overall house advantage is greater than 1.5%. Which means you'll want to avoid slots, keno and the other casino games discussed below.

Slots

Slot machines are one of the biggest money makers for the casinos—which means they are one of the biggest money losers for the player. Nobody in their right mind should play the slots for anything else but pure entertainment...if you consider losing money entertaining. The house edge on the slots is too great to allow a reasonable expectation of profit. Of course, there will always be exceptions to this rule...you've probably heard every one (the casinos make sure of that!). Like the visitor from out of state who parlayed twenty silver dollars into a $250,000 jackpot. It happens. But don't expect it to happen to you.

Normally there is no way to know what the casino edge is on individual slot machines. This is because each machine can be programmed to give the house whatever edge it desires. Machines that return a higher proportion of the player's investment are known as "loose" slots and are more prevalent downtown than on the Vegas Strip. These lower-house-percentage slots also tend to be placed in busy sections of the casino, so more people will witness payoffs to players. The low "vig" machines usually aren't placed next to one another.

Gamblers who are aware of these machine placements

try to confine their play to those casinos known for "loose" slots. They don't play two slots in a row (a common practice), and they concentrate on those machines located in busy sections of the gambling establishment. One slot player I know makes a point of talking with the change girl, informing her she'll receive a "toke" (tip) if he wins on a machine she recommends. These employees are sometimes familiar with the better-paying machines, and my gambling friend hopes she'll point him in the right direction. Sometimes it works. Most of the time it doesn't. You just can't expect to win money at the slots. In the long run, it doesn't happen often enough to make it worth your while.

Permit me one final observation about slot machines. Recently, the casinos introduced a new gimmick in an attempt to convert players from the low cost slots (nickel, dime, quarter) to the dollar machines. What the casinos came up with were "carousels," a special circle of dollar slots, with big payouts and lower house advantages. The casino edge, usually 3 or 4%, is clearly posted for the gambler to see. The "carousels" are a definite improvement from the slot player's point of view. For the first time the house edge can be determined, and it is significantly lower than the 12–50% "vig" levied on other slot machine play. Still, a 3–4% edge is well above the recommended 1.5% level. Thus, I suggest you stay away from the carousels...unless you enjoy being led around in circles and taken for a ride!

Keno

Keno is normally played sitting down...and that's the position most people should be in when they learn what the casino advantage is. Any way you slice it, the house extracts a healthy profit from keno—20% and up, depending on the wager. The game attracts a lot of players because you can win $50,000 on a $1.40 gamble. Don't bet on it happening to you, however. In fact—when it comes to keno—don't bet on it, period.

Other Games

Most casinos feature so-called "side-games," like Chuck-A-Luck, the Big Six dice wheel, and the Wheel of Fortune. These games should be avoided at all costs because of the high costs...to you. As an example, consider the Wheel of Fortune. This money-making gem for the casino should really be installed in psychiatric wards. That way, people who choose to play the thing can have their heads examined at the same time. And well they should—the casino advantage on the money wheel averages close to 25%. Who needs it?! The casino...not you.

Playing Smart Helps You Psych Out Vegas

Playing intelligently at the tables helps you cut down the house advantage to a point where you have a gambling chance of winning. In some cases (e.g., blackjack), it can actually turn the odds in your favor and put the casino at a mathematical disadvantage. What gambler can ask for more?

I can...and so can you...because playing smart helps you in a second crucial way. It makes you feel more competent, confident, clear-headed and capable of self-control. These are feelings that not only help you play more effectively at the tables; they also immunize you against the psychological ploys used by the casinos to encourage poor gambling.

The next time you go to Vegas, go smart. A "no brainer" might be a winning hand in Gin Rummy, but it's a losing style at the tables. Play intelligently and you'll be playing to win.

CHAPTER 9

HOW TO BUILD YOUR OWN
GARAGE IN LAS VEGAS

> "If you'll manage your
> money, you'll manage to
> win."
> —*A Gambler's Motto*

You meet some pretty interesting people in gambling casinos. I remember one individual in particular, a portly, old gentleman named William, who made my acquaintance during a hectic crap game. Perfectly dressed and manicured, he looked every inch the conservative Boston banker...until the dice started rolling. At that moment the image of conservatism went out the window, as he began shouting and wagering with the zeal of a high-roller from Texas.

For an hour we played together, exchanging quips and making money, as the dice stayed hot. Then things cooled off, and I decided to take a break. William didn't. He kept betting like The Last Desperado. . .and I wondered how long his winnings would hold out.

Not long. About half an hour later he wandered into the coffee shop where I was eating, and pulled up a chair.

"How'd you make out?" I asked, already certain of his answer.

My new acquaintance rolled his eyes. "Wiped out. Kaput. You couldn't buy a *pass* out there."

"Maybe you should've left when the dice started missing," I suggested, hoping William wouldn't be offended by my unsolicited advice.

"Perhaps. . ." he responded, thoughtfully. "Seems I never know when to quit."

I decided to press my recommendation further. "Have you ever thought about setting losing and winning limits at the tables?" I paused, studying William's expression for several moments. "Have you ever practiced money management?"

William nodded affirmatively. "Sure, I practice money management. I play until my money runs out."

William was serious. And William was broke.

Playing Smart + Money Management = A Winning Combination

Each of you has two major weapons at your command in the battle against the casino. One weapon is knowledge—knowing how to gamble intelligently. The other is money management—the ability to utilize your financial resources in a manner that maximizes your chances for profit and minimizes your chances of loss.

The two weapons complement each other—they work best together. William, for example, played smart at the tables (he made low house advantage wagers only) but he didn't "lock up" any of his winnings . . . a cardinal principle of good money management.

In this chapter, I'd like to present the principles of effective money management which will help you win in the casino. Like the discussion of "playing smart" in the previous chapter, the emphasis here will be on "psyching out" Vegas, using money management as a weapon to: (1) increase your chances for profit at the tables; and (2) immunize you against casino ploys designed to encourage poor gambling.

Before I can do this, however, I want you to think carefully before answering the following question:

Why Do You Want To Gamble?

The reason I ask you this question is because your answer will determine your money management strategy.

If your answer to the question is: "I want to gamble to make a profit," then your money management strategy becomes incredibly simple. What you should do is take all the money you ever intend to gamble in a casino, place it on the lowest house advantage wager you can find, and await the outcome.[19] If you lose . . . well, so much for your gambling career . . . at least you have the satisfaction of knowing you gave yourself the best mathematical shot at the casino bankroll. If you win . . . well, so much for your gambling career . . . you should take the money and run, because any further bets will decrease your mathematical expectation for maximum profit.

"Hey . . . wait a minute!" you say. "What fun is it to go

all the way to Vegas to place one bet? Of course I want to win . . . but I also want to play."

Well, now, that's an entirely different matter . . . and this is where the concepts of money management get interesting.

Here's the problem: in any casino game the percentage favors the house[20]—the greater the number of wagers you make, the greater the chances become for the casino to win your money. Of course, the more wagers you make, the more time it will take for this to happen. And therein lies the rub: *if you want the best possible chance of making a profit, then you should make one bet with your total bankroll; on the other hand, if you want the longest possible time to play at the tables, you should break your bankroll into as many bets as possible.*

Obviously, *your* optimal money management strategy will be determined by what *you* want out of gambling: more time at the tables or more money in your pocket. Most of us will probably want both (no wonder most people think gamblers are wacky). Therefore, I am going to present a money management strategy aimed at giving you a chance for both action *and* profits at the tables. By necessity, mine is a "middle ground" strategy—it *won't* give you the best chance of winning, nor will it give you the best chance of staying the longest possible time at the tables. *What it will give you is a reasonable chance of winning with a reasonable amount of playing time.* Because that is, in the final analysis, what most people really want out of gambling.[21]

Some Guidelines for
Sound Money Management

When it comes to psychological warfare between gambler and casino, the fiercest struggle centers on the money management battlefield. The casino owners reap their biggest profits from players who abandon sound money management precepts, then plunge into action with chips flying. Thus, Vegas has been designed to "psych" gamblers into "blowing" their money away. To effectively counter this casino offensive you *must* learn about *and use* money management at the tables. This is a primary requirement for psyching out Vegas and giving yourself a shot at the casino's coffers.

Being an effective money manager in Vegas is really a two-part process. There are steps you must take before you depart on your gambling trip, and then there are rules to follow once you begin play at the tables. For the sake of clarity I am going to consider each part of the process separately.

Money Management Steps to Take
Before You Embark on a Gambling Trip

Your first and most basic step in a sound money management program is: *determine how much you intend to gamble.* How much you *intend* to gamble should never exceed how much you can *afford* to gamble. *Never risk in action more than you can comfortably afford to lose.*

There are two reasons for this. One is obvious: when you start betting amounts that, if lost, could severely deplete your financial resources . . . you are courting personal hardship and heartache. Don't do it! No gambling thrill is worth the destruction of your financial security. The second reason is not so obvious, but it's vitally important to your play at the tables. If you gamble more than you can comfortably afford to lose, there is a good chance it will affect your judgment during play. You're betting what the professionals refer to as "scared money" . . . money you can't afford to lose . . . and when this happens, clear, rational action is often impaired. The professionals have a motto: "Scared money runs away every time." Don't bet beyond your means . . . keep your cash happy, and at home.

You might think that gamblers wouldn't want to risk more than they could comfortably afford to lose. Unfortunately, some do. For these players, their thrill in gambling comes from wagering amounts which involve significant risks to their financial well-being. This is sick gambling. It is the loser's way to bet.

Most of us want to bet enough to make the action "interesting." And, certainly, a person who makes $100,000 a year might find a $1.00 bet less interesting than the individual who brings home $5,000 annually. That is why each of your must decide (based on your financial resources) what constitutes a "reasonable" gambling stake. It is all right to make that stake large enough to keep the wagers exciting, but it should never be so large as to threaten your financial health if you should lose.

Once you have determined the size of your gambling stake, you're ready to take the second step to sound money management: *budgeting that stake over the length of your stay in Vegas*. To do this you must decide in advance the number of times you intend to gamble in the casinos. I strongly recommend you base your figures on a per-day, rather than per-trip, estimate . . . otherwise you might use up all your gambling sessions on the day you arrive and. . .if you lose. . .all your funds will be used up as well.

Let us assume you are going on a two-night, three-day Vegas trip. You would then ask yourself: how many times do I want to play at the tables per day? Suppose your answer is three times a day. (This is a good figure for a three-day trip. Nine or ten gambling sessions per Vegas trip is about optimal.) Then you would multiply the number of sessions per day (3) times the number of days on your trip (3), to come up with your total number of gambling sessions (9). If you intend to refrain from gambling one or more days, you should take that into consideration in your calculations.

Once you have determined the total number of gambling sessions for your trip, you would then divide that number (9) into your total gambling stake, whatever that is. The answer becomes your *per-session stake*. For example, if you had set your total stake at $900, then your per-session stake would be $100 ($900 divided by 9 sessions = $100 per session).

Having selected what your total stake and per-session stake limits will be, you must stick by those limits on your trip. Do not change them in the heat of action at the tables. Deciding to raise your total stake limit, or borrowing against future sessions to finance a current one is the bane of many gamblers, and it spells total destruction for any effective money management strategy. (Incidentally, it is alright to gamble more sessions than you originally decided upon, but only when they are financed out of monies left over from earlier sessions where you either won or broke even. More on this later.)

Do not—I repeat—*do not* alter the limits you have set for yourself. It is here that self-control plays such an important role in winning or losing. If you falter, the casino becomes the overwhelming favorite to wipe you out. If you hold firm, you've got a gambling chance of winning.

Sticking to your limits won't be easy. Vegas has been designed to encourage limit-breaking, and the dream merchants will use every psychological ploy to destroy your self-control. But you have some weapons, too. Later in this chapter I will provide you with a plan to help you combat the casinos and keep your self-imposed limits intact. If you follow the plan, you should be able to psych out Vegas and manage your money effectively. For now, just remember to set reasonable limits for yourself at the tables... and stick by those limits at all costs.

Keeping your stakes well in mind, we're now ready to move to step three in your money management program: *sizing your bets at the tables.* How large should your wagers be?

(1) The bets should be large enough to make them interesting yet give you a chance for a meaningful win;

(2) The bets should be small enough to provide meaningful playing time at the tables and allow you to weather most runs of adverse results should they occur.

These two points are in keeping with a strategy in which we are not betting for maximum profits or maximum time at the tables but rather, a reasonable chance of winning with a reasonable amount of playing time.

I am going to recommend that your original wager for a gambling session be between 2-3% of your allotted bankroll for that session. Thus, if you have a $100 stake for a particular session, the size of your starting wager would be in the $2.00-$3.00 range. Should you begin winning at the table, you may choose to raise your bets as your bankroll increases... but the percentage of the bet to your bankroll size should stay pretty much in the

2-3% range. Thus, if your $100 bankroll balloons to $200, then you could wager between $4.00 and $6.00. You may also choose to decrease your bet if your initial bankroll shrinks . . . again, this is optional.

My bet-sizing recommendations should be viewed as general guidelines, not fixed rules. In the final analysis you should bet an amount that feels most comfortable for you, within the boundaries of the available money you have to spend. If you want to bet higher than the 2-3% figure I have suggested, this is O.K. But you should realize that your chances of being wiped out increase along with your opportunities for greater profit.

We arrive now at the fourth and final step in developing your sound money management strategy: *determining how much you are willing to win or lose gambling in Las Vegas.*

We already know the amount you are willing to lose: the bankroll (total stake) you are bringing along on your trip. It is highly unlikely you will lose all of this money if you gamble intelligently and psych out the casinos as per my instructions . . . yet, it is a possibility which must be included in your calculations. That is why I cautioned you against bringing more money to Vegas than you could comfortably afford to lose.

What would it take to lose your total stake for the trip? Assuming you played correctly—it would take one hell of an adverse run at the tables. Remember, you are dividing your total bankroll into approximately ten parts to stake individual sessions at the tables. *That means you would have to lose your total per-session stake ten times in a row to go home wiped out.* That just doesn't happen very often!

One way to keep gambling losses to a minimum is to send any money home that remains after an individual gambling session is completed. That way, it won't be put back into action where the potential for loss exists. I'll be discussing this option at the end of this chapter, in the section subtitled "Take the Money and Run."

Now to a more pleasant topic . . . winning. When I ask you to determine how much you are willing to win in Vegas, I really mean: "How much money will you have to win before you're willing to say 'I've won enough,' then stop gambling for a given session and/or the entire trip?"

What I am asking you to do here is to think about setting a *winning limit*—a point where you will stop gambling once your win goal has been reached. After all, you've set a losing limit . . . why not a winning limit as well? This might seem nonsensical . . . but it isn't. Most gambling experts agree that win limits are as important as loss limits if you want to attack the casino coffers successfully. This is because both limits work to cut your losses in Vegas. The loss rule does this by limiting the amount of money you can lose at the tables; the win rule does it by limiting the amount of money you can lose *back* to the tables.

I set my winning limit on a per-session and total-trip basis, and I recommend you do the same. How much an individual has to win before he feels satisfied enough to stop gambling is a highly personal decision and one you'll have to make for yourself. I'll tell you what my limits are, however, if you want to use them as guidelines.

I end a gambling session whenever I win half my stake for that particular session. Thus, if I have alloted $500 for a particular session, and I win $250, I quit. That means I leave the table with $750 in chips. I end my gambling on a trip whenever I win half of my total gambling stake for that particular trip. Thus, if I have allotted $5,000 for my total gambling stake on the trip, and I win $2,500, I quit playing for the rest of that trip. That means I leave Las Vegas with $7,500.

I feel this win limit is realistic—it isn't so high that winning sessions are impossible; yet, it isn't so low that winning sessions are meaningless.

At this point some of you are probably thinking: "Ahhh, Karlins is crazy . . . doesn't he know the old saying, 'Cut your losses by letting your winnings run'? It's hard enough to win in the first place . . . who wants to cut the streak short?"

Here is my answer to that very reasonable question. When I say "quit winners," I don't mean quit right in the middle of a hand, or a roll, or a deal, or what have you. If I am at the dice table and the shooter is in the middle of a hot roll—I wait until that roll ends before I pick up my chips . . . even though I might have hit my win limit well before the shooter finally sevened-out.

If you're at a table where things are hot, by all means stay there as long as you keep winning . . . no matter how far over your win limit that puts you. But the FIRST time you lose . . . get the hell away from the table and take your winnings with you!

Money Management Rules to Follow at the Tables

All right. You've determined your total-trip bankroll, established your per-session stakes, sized your bets and decided on your winning and losing limits. You've also remembered to get on the plane, and now you're in Vegas, ready to gamble. What now?

Now it's time to implement your four money management steps with action at the tables. You will be able to do this effectively if you follow the wagering rules I am going to present. Maybe it would be better if I referred to these rules as "guidelines." Many players don't like to follow rules, they want to be "spontaneous"...free to play their hunches and change their limits at will. I understand their feelings—I used to bet that way myself. It is fun, but it is also costly. For most of these players, being "spontaneous" translates into "lacking self-control."

So I'm going to stick with the word "rules." If you want to bend these rules a bit...go ahead. You've got to do what's comfortable for you at the tables. But in doing so, please consider that these rules were designed to give you the best possible chance of winning in the casino. If you choose to alter or ignore them, you do so at your own peril!

(1)   Never bet "scared" money...money you cannot comfortably afford to lose. Doing so can adversely affect your play...and your life.

(2)   Once you have established a gambling limit, stick to it at all costs. That goes for your total-trip bankroll, as well as your per-session stakes. It also includes any winning and losing limits you have set for yourself.

(3)   Once you have determined your total-trip bankroll, bring only that amount of money with you to Vegas. Make sure there is no way you can get additional funds for gambling while you are there.

(4)   Bring only your allotted stake to each gambling session. Keep any other funds as far away from the casino as possible. That way you'll have a margin of safety should your self-control falter.

(5)   The size of your wager should be determined by the

size of your bankroll at the tables. A bet size that is 2-3% of that bankroll is recommended.

(6) Never, never increase your bets when losing. Breaking this rule is a surefire ticket to the poorhouse. Don't chase your losses: a bad losing streak can outlast the financial resources of even the richest gamblers.

(7) If you want to bet higher, or more frequently, do so only when you are winning. That way you will be gambling with "casino money."

(8) Play to win . . . but don't be greedy. As one authority put it: "Don't go for the chandeliers."

(9) If you lose five bets in a row, leave the table at once. This "consecutive loss" rule is designed to get you away from the tables before you lose your temper, and possibly your self-control as well. Nothing is more frustrating to a gambler than a string of losses. Losing time after time is no fun . . . and can, in fact, affect your judgment. So leave and come back later, clear of head and refreshed in spirit.

(10) If you're losing during a gambling session, don't become despondent and give up hope. Comebacks are always possible.

(11) If you do lose at a gambling session, put it out of your mind before you gamble again. Each session is a "whole new ballgame," and you should not let previous session experiences affect your current play.

(12) Don't stay at the tables too long. An hour per session is about optimal . . . playing longer tends to dull your alertness, and gives the house percentage more opportunity to work on your bankroll.

(13) Never make a bet to cover costs that aren't related to gambling—e.g., dinner, show tickets, cab fare.

(14) Play only when you feel mentally and physically alert.

(15) Stop gambling immediately if your feel hassled or emotionally distraught for any reason.

(16) Keep track of all your bets and make sure your payoffs are correct.

(17) Avoid establishing or utilizing casino credit. Using this type of credit gives the casino management more opportunity to psych you out. When you have ready credit, there is always the temptation to use more than you should, even to the point of asking for additional funds once your per-session stake is exhausted (see Rule 4). Also, there is the possibility of increasing your credit *ceiling*, a request you might make in the heat of play...then regret later on. When you play at the tables, don't sign markers. Bring cash instead...it will help keep things in a more realistic perspective.

Take the Money and Run

You now have some steps and rules which, if properly followed, should give you a gambling chance of winning. So, let's say that you do. You're in Vegas and you've just won a pocketful of cash in your very first gambling session.

Now what? Now that money is starting to burn a hole in your pocket! In Vegas, money buys you action...and action is beckoning from every direction. And suddenly you come face-to-face with a phenomenon unique to gambling towns:

Winning money at the tables is only half the battle. You're not a total winner until you get the money out of town and safely home.

Don't worry. I have a plan to help you accomplish just that.

My plan centers on a concept known as "garaging." Originally the term referred to the winning gambler who "garaged" his original stake and, under no circumstances, would he break into it. As you will soon see, I use the term more broadly: here it refers to any gambling monies (capital) that are taken out of action and sent home.

If you follow the procedures I set forth, and don't yield to the myriad temptations designed to part you from your bankroll...your gambling money should last longer, and your self-esteem should grow stronger. Do not think that garaging will be easy: we have seen how self-control in Las Vegas is a difficult objective to achieve. But it *can* be achieved...and *must be* if you want to build garages instead of casinos in Las Vegas.

How to Garage Your Money
Before You Leave on Your Trip

PHASE 1: Decide how much money you want to risk in action at the casinos during your trip (your total bankroll).

PHASE 2: Once you have determined the size of your total bankroll, go out and purchase a set of travelers checks for that amount. The denomination of the travelers check should be in a 1:50 ratio to your total gambling stake (Example: if your stake is $5,000, purchase fifty $100 travelers checks; if your stake is $500, purchase fifty $10 checks, etc.). Do NOT substitute cashiers checks or postal money orders for the travelers checks...they have drawbacks that limit effective garaging. Also, do NOT come out to Vegas and play off a casino credit line: this will totally destroy the effectiveness of the garaging system.

PHASE 3: Purchase fifty personal-size envelopes (they can be comfortably carried in a purse or sportcoat pocket), address them to yourself, stamp them and—if you're paranoid—place a sheet of folded-up paper inside each one. For record-keeping purposes, you might also want to number each envelope, placing the number on the *inside* lip of the envelope. Place a rubber band around the envelopes, then pack them in your suitcase. (You probably won't use all the envelopes on one trip. If not, you can always use them on subsequent visits. The important thing is to not run short of envelopes while you're in Las Vegas.)

PHASE 4: Decide how many *gambling days* will occur on your trip. Count only those days you intend to gamble (Example: if you'll be in Las Vegas five days, but don't intend to gamble the first day you arrive, then you'll have four gambling days). Then divide your gambling stake equally over the gambling days. (Example: Your stake is $2,000. You intend to gamble four days. Your daily gambling allotment would be $500).

PHASE 5: Decide how many *gambling sessions* you would like each day. Then divide your daily gambling stake equally among the allotted sessions. (Example: Your daily stake is $500; you intend to gamble once in the morning and once in the evening. Your per-session gambling stake is $250.)

PHASE 6: As much as possible, pay for all nongambling trip expenses in advance. Plane fares, hotel rooms, rental cars...all these items can be booked and pre-paid through a travel agent. Many of the hotels offer total packages, which will allow you to pay in advance for everything from meals, to shows, to gratuities.

PHASE 7: Before you depart on your trip, make sure you divest yourself of any credit cards, casino credit lines, checks, or other sources of potential currency that could be used for gambling in Las Vegas. Ideally, you are now in a position whereby the only money you can use will be the travelers checks you bring. Please note: you may bring (for emergencies) a small amount of cash to take care of such things as cabs, tips, etc. But do keep track of this money, and don't use it for gambling. Also, if you feel uncomfortable traveling without credit cards...or if you anticipate a lot of non-gambling expenses (e.g., shows outside your hotel), then carry only those credit cards that *don't* provide cash advances.

When You Arrive in Las Vegas

PHASE 8: Open a safe deposit box. All major hotels have them. They are normally located near the cashiers cage in the casino. Place your envelopes and travelers checks in your box, so they will be readily available on a 24-hour basis.

When You Gamble

PHASE 9: Restrict your gambling to those games and bets where the casino advantage is 1.5% or less.

PHASE 10: When gambling, observe the rules of money management discussed in this chapter.

PHASE 11: Before each gaming session, go to your safe deposit box. Cash only the number of travelers checks necessary to reach the proper stake for that session.

One note of caution, however. If you don't play blackjack properly it can become a highly favorable game *for the house*. The casino edge at blackjack rises dramatically as player sophistication drops. Unfortunately, many gamblers don't realize this. They browse through a book on the topic...get a few hints from a friend...play a few hands at the kitchen table...then blow into Vegas ready to make a fortune. More often than not, they're blown right back out, poorer and (hopefully) wiser for their efforts. (Just to get you started on the right track, I've included some information on Basic Strategy, along with easy-to-read charts, in the next section.)

Going up against a casino with a little knowledge about blackjack is like challenging an NFL lineman to a fight with a little knowledge about boxing. Forget it, you're going to get your ears pinned back! The reason why the casinos love all the publicity about blackjack being "beatable" is because they know most players won't have the patience, knowledge, mental skills and "psyching" abilities to pull off any significant wins.

If blackjack wasn't a continuing money-winner for the casinos, it wouldn't be played. Period. You would do well to keep that fact in mind. Blackjack can be beaten, but most gamblers won't be able to do it. If you want to be one of the wealthier minority, then take time to read some of the texts I will be recommending in Appendix A, spend a lot of time learning and practicing proper play and, finally, utilize the "psyching" principles I'm teaching you. Please recall the comment from the Las Vegas blackjack dealer, which introduced the first chapter of this book:

> "Ever wonder why I'm still dealing a game
> that can be beat? Because percentages aren't
> the whole story. There's the mental factor. I
> don't care how well the player can count

Take the money to the tables and begin play. If, during a gaming session, you run out of your allotted money . . . you must stop immediately and *not play again until your next scheduled session*. At no time should you go to your safe deposit box and take out additional money so you can continue play at a session where your allotted funds have been exhausted. (Taking only the allotted amount of money to each gaming session should help you avoid the temptation to "steam." The urge to chase losses is far greater when you can simply reach into your pocket for more cash. Once you have to leave the table to retrieve more funds, the desire to splurge dissipates, and cooler heads prevail.)

PHASE 12: Once you have completed a gaming session, cash in any chips you have, and note the total. At this point you have your choice of following either PHASE 12A—the "conservative" garaging approach—or PHASE 12B—the "liberal" garaging rule. Obviously, those who follow PHASE 12A will be more likely to have money waiting for them when they return home. Those who follow PHASE 12B will probably see more action at the tables.

PHASE 12A: Take all the money you have left after cashing in, and send it home immediately! Here's an example to show you how to do it. Let us assume your original session stake was $500, and you won an additional $200. Thus, you have $700 in cash. You would go to your safe deposit box, take out a mailing envelope and seven hundred dollars worth of travelers checks. DO NOT SIGN THE TRAVELERS CHECKS A SECOND TIME. Rather, place them directly in the envelope, seal it, and drop it in the nearest mailbox. Place the $700 cash in the safe deposit box, and lock it up. Then, when your next session begins, take $500 in cash out of the box and use in at the tables. At the end of that session, take whatever money is left, go back to your box and repeat the process of sending out travelers checks in the amount equal to the cash remaining at the session's end. (This is one of the great advantages of using travelers checks. You have them ready to send home...they are safe...and you don't have to worry about changing cash into money orders, etc., after each gaming session. After all, the faster you get your funds in the mail...the less likely they'll go back on the tables.) If, at any time during your trip, you find that you have sent home all your travelers checks, then, at the end of each subsequent session, take what cash you have left, change it into travelers checks, and send those home—even on a Sunday (an American Express office is open Sundays in Las Vegas). To be on the safe side, keep a record of all travelers checks sent home. That way, if any are lost in the mail, it will be easier for you to get refunds.

PHASE 12B: As in PHASE 12A, count your money after cashing in your chips at the end of a gaming session. If you have won any money, take this amount and send it home immediately, as per instructions in PHASE 12A. Your original stake for the session can either be sent home as well (as in PHASE 12A), or kept in the safe deposit box for an extra gambling session. *Extra gambling sessions are allowed only with monies not lost in earlier sessions.* In this way, the player does not violate PHASES 4&5 (see also PHASE 13 below). If you *lose* money during the session, then send home whatever remains from your starting pre-session stake (as per PHASE 12A), and start your next session with a new stake.

PHASE 13: If, at the end of a gambling day, you have any of that day's gambling stake left over (see PHASE 4), it must be sent home immediately...as per instructions in PHASE 12A. PHASE 13 is predicated on the proper balance between saving money and being "in the action." The reasoning goes as follows: each gambling day is, in a sense, a gambling trip in itself. During each day the player has a minimum number of gambling sessions guaranteed (those already determined before the trip began . . . see PHASE 5), plus any additional ones undertaken with funds not lost in the guaranteed sessions (see PHASE 12B). Therefore, if a player chooses to go to bed with some of his daily gambling allotment remaining . . . one must assume his need for action was satisfied that day, and any remaining monies should be garaged and saved for some future trip.

PHASE 14: If you reach a winning limit for a session or trip, stop gambling at once, send the money home as per instructions in PHASE 12A. Then drink a toast to your skill and self control!

* * *

There you have it: fourteen steps to help you garage your money in Las Vegas. Taken together, they represent a viable system of money management that will keep losses down when the tables "go cold," and winnings intact when things are going your way. There is no "magic" to my plan—it won't change the odds at the tables—but it will provide you with a powerful tool for self-control. Think of it as your psychological shield—and use it to protect yourself against the psychological warfare waged by the casinos.

In a gaming casino, you're encouraged to lose. This is the psychology of Las Vegas . . . a psychology that keeps turning winners into losers. With my garaging system, you're encouraged to win; in fact, you're even encouraged for breaking even and/or conserving as much of your initial stake as possible. Each of the fourteen steps is carefully designed to get your money in and out of Las Vegas as smoothly and quickly as possible. The idea of having travelers checks and stamped envelopes ready for immediate mailing serves two purposes: (1) it provides an immediate reward for the player... who can readily see (with pride) his money going home and not into the casino coffers; (2) it gets funds sent home FAST, eliminating the need to carry the cash around town for hours before it reaches the post office.

I cannot emphasize strongly enough the need to get your homebound funds out of Vegas quickly. The longer you hold onto your money, the greater the temptation will be to put it back into action.

Remember the gauntlet? It's a double line of men armed with clubs and they beat a person who is forced to run between them. Think of the Las Vegas Strip that way. Casinos line each side of the street, ready to beat you out of your money. Just how long do you think you can run the gauntlet without losing your stake?

Once you become accustomed to the garaging system, I think you will find it not only profitable but an *enjoyable* part of your gambling experience. What, on paper, seems like a chore... running back and forth from tables to safe deposit box, putting travelers checks in envelopes, dropping the envelopes in the mail... becomes, in practice, a joy.

To me, each envelope mailed becomes a victory over the tables—proof-positive that I could beat the Las Vegas "psychout" and come home to find money in my mailbox.

The next time you're in Vegas—or any other gambling town—why not try my garaging plan? At a minimum, it will make you more aware of your cash flow and the casino procedures that encourage losing; at best, it will give you a vehicle for sound money management at the tables.

Go ahead...build your garage in Las Vegas. And while you're at it, you might want to build a larger mailbox back home, too.

CHAPTER 10

THEY BEAT THE CASINOS...
YOU CAN, TOO!

"Casino games were created
by human minds; they can be
beaten by human minds."
—*A Vegas Blackjack Counter*

Up to this point we have done a lot of talking about how to win in Vegas: how to play smart, how to manage money properly, how to psych out the casinos, etc. In this chapter, I want to bring you the stories of some gambling pioneers who have already been winners there. Some of their winning techniques have been unorthodox... but all of them have been brilliant assaults on the casino coffers.
casino coffers.

In each case, these pioneers devised methods to beat games that everyone thought couldn't be beaten.

This chapter is, by the very nature of its subject matter, open-ended. New techniques of winning are currently being developed in the minds of gamblers world-wide...and new assaults on the casino banks will be forthcoming as long as dice are rolled or cards are dealt.

It is a tribute to the ingenuity and persistence of gamblers that they have found ways to turn the house percentages around...to gain the winning edge at the tables. Who knows—maybe one of you reading this book might be the next innovator of a winning attack on the casinos.

When you read about the gamblers in this chapter, please keep in mind that they were able to beat the house because they found ways to make the mathematical odds go in their favor. As long as the mathematical edge remains with the casino, the player should expect to lose *in the long run*. In the short run, however, anything can happen...especially with smart play and effective money management. And that's what psyching out Vegas is all about.

Goliath Takes a Tumble

The biblical antics of slingshot-wielding David strike a responsive chord in most of us, gamblers in particular. The idea of a courageous lad going against the odds, facing the mighty resources of the awesome Goliath with little more than a pebble and a sense of conviction, really warms the cockles of a gamer's heart. And why not? The player has been there himself! He knows all about mismatches—he has entered the huge den of his opponent and matched his few puny chips against the vast resources and house percentage of the juggernaut casino. And he knows what it feels like to turn his pants pockets inside out—the gambler's white flag of surrender.

No, the casino is not easily beaten. Yet, a few enterprising "Davids" have locked horns with the house and won (and their numbers are increasing). In fact, the study of gambling history documents this startling find: *every major casino game has already been beaten.*

How was it done? How can *you* do it? To answer these questions let us journey to the land of the giant-killers, where we will meet some very unusual gamblers doing some very ingenious things at the gaming tables.

The first stop on our journey will be the blackjack tables, where the most celebrated gambling coups have taken—and continue to take—place. Then it's on to the studied elegance of the baccarat layout, replete with high-fashion dealers and high-limit bets. What journey would be complete without a stop at the whirling roulette wheel, the ricocheting sound of the ivory ball recalling a thousand legends of fortunes won and lost? We will pause there to recount some spectacular coups and then move on to our final destination, the crap tables. There, amidst the calls of the stickman, the shouts of the players, and the tumbling dice, we will uncover a few more modern "Davids" who, like their predecessor, attempted to dispatch their adversary with the flick of a wrist.

Throughout our journey I will be providing reading references for those of you who think you might want to become contemporary "Davids" by taking a shot at beating the house. If you are one of these people, let me add my usual cautionary note before you go off and begin loading your slingshot. Beating the casino is not easy; if it were, there would be no casinos. Mastering the techniques discussed in these pages takes a lot of patience and time, not to mention skill. Learning to disguise your play so the casino cannot uncover your winning ways is also important. But more of this later. Now, let the journey begin!

Blackjack

The 1950s. Most people fondly remember the decade as a simpler, slower-paced America; the era of *Grease* and *American Graffiti*. Knowledgeable gamblers, however, remember it fondly for another reason: it was during these years that the first steps to winning blackjack were taken. At the Atomic Energy Commission's laboratory at Los Alamos, and in Maryland, at the Army's Aberdeen Proving Ground...scientists were hard at work—using primitive computers to design a weapon of a different sort, a weapon that could blast the casino blackjack advantage right off the map!

And what was this weapon? The development of an optimal playing strategy, a strategy that "came into its own" when the celebrated work of Professor Edward Thorp, the greatest casino giant-killer of them all, was published. In his well known book, *Beat the Dealer*, Thorp provided the player with a "decision matrix"—a set of rules which allowed him to play each hand in the best possible way (giving him the highest probable chance of winning.)

The Thorp system recognized that a gambler's playing strategy should be based on the cards remaining in the deck; that is, playing strategy should be varied as the cards are dealt out and the composition of the deck changes. For this reason, Thorp instructed the gambler to keep track of the cards ("count" them), so he would know when the deck was "favorable" (had an abundance of 10's and aces—cards that increase the player's chances of winning), or "unfavorable" (had a higher proportion of unfavorable cards—like 5's—which decrease the probability of his beating the dealer).

Thorp also outlined principles of money management and bet sizing which helped the gambler take full advantage of favorable situations, at those moments when the composition of the deck favored the player over the house. To illustrate, the player was instructed to make a larger bet when the deck was favorable (a condition in which the player won a higher percentage of the wagers), and a smaller bet when the deck was unfavorable (a condition in which the player lost a higher percentage of the wagers). The net effect was an increase in revenue for the player. The card counter could also adjust his playing strategy for each hand (e.g., hit, stand, double down, split) in accordance with the composition of the unplayed deck—enhancing his overall chances of winning.

Beat the Dealer is probably the best-known book on gambling in America today. It has undeniably presented a winning strategy for beating the casinos, for slaying Goliath. Further, since its publication, other authors have written texts that contain even more powerful playing strategies for winning at 21. Some of these books are listed in Appendix A.

What has been the result of all this? In monetary terms, blackjack "counters" have taken millions of dollars out of casino coffers. A few of them have even become rich and famous. One such individual is Ken Uston, who chronicles his rise to success in his books, *The Big Player* and *Million Dollar Blackjack*.

There is absolutely no question . . . blackjack can be beaten, it has been beaten, and continues to be beaten. Well, then, why haven't the games closed down? Why is the Casino-Goliath still standing? There are several answers. For one, casinos have seen fit to bar those players who are particularly troublesome (i.e., those who win too much money), thus reducing the threat to their banks. Further, casinos have created playing conditions that make counting more difficult and/or less effective—for example, four decks are used rather than one, and the cards are shuffled every few hands.

Yet, it is NOT the use of gaming countermeasures such as these that have saved the day for the casino owners. In reality, these countermeasures are relatively mild—a good player can get around them with ease. The real reason casinos continue to profit from blackjack—even when strategies for beating the tables have been available for twenty years—is because most players cannot, or will not, use these strategies properly.

Some players just are not intelligent or quick enough to count the cards accurately, particularly when they're in the imposing casino environment. The owners realize this and do their part in making the player's task more difficult: they employ fast dealers, supply free drinks, and the like.

Other players *could* be effective counters—they have the brains for it—but they don't take the necessary time to learn the strategy well. These gamblers are basically lazy; they figure a night or two at the kitchen table with a deck of cards should make them accomplished "case-down" players. (Case-down players are able to rapidly count down the deck.) It is certainly safe to say that casino monies lost to "expert" counters have been reimbursed many times over by the legions of "would be" counters who come ill-prepared to the tables—ready to make a killing—but who end up blowing their bankrolls in the process. It is no wonder casino bosses lick their chops when they see a weekend gambler show up at the tables . . . a slightly used copy of Thorp in one hand, and a fistfull of cash in the other. Counting cards is just not that easy, and those who think otherwise will soon find their egos and their wallets flattened.

Those players who cannot count cards, and those who can but won't practice enough to be effective, help explain why blackjack is still dealt in casinos. The other reason the game is alive and well is much more tragic, because it involves players whose weaknesses are far more difficult to excuse than those of the gambler who loses because he is lazy or has a poor memory. For instance:

(1)   Players who know the game can be beaten, but play to lose, because they *want* to lose. These are the people who should be barred from the casinos, before they are ruined financially. (A complete description of this type of gambler will be found in Chapter 18.)

(2)   Players who know the game can be beaten and, therefore, pass it up because it "isn't a challenge" or it "takes the fun out of the game." There are lots of these gamblers in the casinos. You can identify them by their comments, statements like, "Who wants to play blackjack?... It's like a job, just like working"....or, "Who wants to be the second person to climb Mt. Everest?"

(3)   Players who know how to beat the game but can't seem to do it in the casino. They perform perfectly in their kitchens using matchsticks—but when they play for "meaningful money" in the casino, they "choke"—and their performance deteriorates.

(4)   Players who follow the proper strategy while they're ahead, but fall apart in the face of a losing sequence. Even expert case-down players have been known to lose control during a run of bad cards, throwing strategy to the wind, "steaming," and losing their stakes in the process.

(5)   Players who succumb to temptations which make their play ineffective. The primary temptation is, of

course, alcohol—always within easy reach in American casinos. It can reduce the finest counter to the level of a bumbling novice, making him easy prey for the "jaws of averages."

(6) Players who know how to beat the game, but make their card counting so obvious that they are barred from the casinos. (If you want to count and not be harrassed, you will have to camouflage your activity. More on this in Chapter 11.)

So much for why people can't win at blackjack. What about those who think they can? Like you. What can you do to "beat the dealer"? Here are my recommendations.

First: make sure you don't have any of the playing characteristics of the gamblers I've just finished describing. If you do, change them, or don't expect to win at blackjack.

Second: learn how to beat the game. There are some excellent books to get you on the right track, and I've included them in Appendix A. If you'd prefer to learn in a classroom-type setting, then you might consider attending the Stanley Roberts School of Winning Blackjack, which is available in several major American cities.

Third: practice, practice, practice. Get to the point where card counting, playing strategy and bet sizing are second nature, automatic, instantaneous. I suggest you begin your practice at home, where mistakes won't be costly. Then move on to the casino, playing for *very small* stakes while you perfect your game.

Fourth: learn proper methods of camouflage; that is, learn to disguise your play so the dealers and pit bosses will not suspect you of being a counter (see Chapter 11). Learning to count cards is only half the battle—not getting barred from the casino is the other factor gamblers must contend with. Always remember: you can't win if you can't play!

If you follow my four recommendations faithfully, there is no reason you can't beat blackjack and join the legions of "Davids" who are battering the "Casino-Goliaths" across the green felt battleground.

Baccarat

Could card counting procedures, so effective in giving the player an edge in blackjack, work in the plush, big money game of baccarat? This question has intrigued several mathematically-gifted investigators, including Edward Thorp and Allan N. Wilson.

In his book, *The Casino Gambler's Guide* (which, by the the way, I recommend as one of the best single reference books on casino gambling), Wilson tells of a baccarat coup using card counting methods. The coup in question was pulled off by Dr. Thorp and a partner who made side bets that the banker's two-card total would be 9 or 8. These two bets carried a 9:1 payoff, with a house advantage of approximately 5%. They made these bets when their card count indicated conditions were favorable for a 9 or 8 to occur. This was no easy task: to locate these favorable conditions required counting down to nearly the bottom of *eight* baccarat decks, where the favorable betting conditions could be identified. Further, even when the Herculean case-down was accomplished, favorable circumstances for betting didn't occur that often ...only about 10% of the time.

Using their counting techniques, Thorp and his colleague won several thousand dollars. The casinos were not too happy about this—and, because it is difficult to disguise counting procedures when you're waiting till the end of eight decks to make any sizeable bets, the pit bosses were quick to catch on to what was happening. The result? They weren't very receptive to the good Doctor and his companion. One casino simply barred them from play. Another eliminated side betting. So much for that coup.

What about the possibility of beating baccarat today? Can it be done? On the "main bets"—player and banker —it seems unlikely.

TABLE 10-1
Frequency of Baccarat Starting Hands, Using Six Decks

Two-Card Hand Total	Combinations	Percent of Total	Chance in One Hand
0	7,140	14.71	6.80
1	4,608	9.50	10.52
2	4,584	9.44	10.58
3	4,608	9.50	10.58
4	4,584	9.44	10.58
5	4,608	9.50	10.52
6	4,584	9.44	10.58
7	4,608	9.50	10.52
8	4,584	9.44	10.58
9	4,608	9.50	10.52
Totals	48,516	100.00	

Chart shows frequency of hitting various hands in baccarat, along with the chance of winning in one hand with a "natural" 8 or 9.

As author Wilson points out, "...the hitch lies in the fact that the game is too 'balanced' ...Blackjack is much less symmetrical."[22] As far as the "side bets" are concerned, if you can still find them, it might be possible to do a little giant-killing—but the card counting is so arduous, camouflage so difficult, and the opportunities for favorable conditions so rare, that it just doesn't seem worth the effort. The way I see it, the player would be better advised to spend his time learning card counting at blackjack where the profit potential is higher, favorable betting conditions more frequent, and camouflage more easily accomplished.

Roulette

When it comes to winning and losing at roulette, the bottom line is very simple, indeed: over the long run casinos win and players lose because the game has a built-in "house percentage" that makes it, in a mathematical sense, "unfair" to the gambler.

How unfair? In America, using primarily the double-zero wheel, the house extracts about 5¼% for the privilege of playing. In places that use the single-zero "European" wheel, the house edge is cut to half that amount (2.70%). When the single-zero wheel is combined with the *"en prison"* feature, the casino percentage (on even money bets) drops to a more reasonable 1.35%, which is better than a player can get making line bets (without odds) at the crap tables.

How can a player hope to win at roulette? By overcoming this house advantage—by finding some way of swinging the mathematical percentages in his favor. For a double-zero wheel, the player will have to find some method to overcome the normal 5.26% casino edge. For "European" wheels, with their lower house advantage, the percentages a player has to overcome will be smaller.

Beating *any* roulette wheel—even those with the smaller house edge—is an awesome assignment. That hasn't, of course, deterred many gamblers from trying. In fact, more players have probably tried to "beat the wheel" than any other casino table game. Now, here's the good news: some have succeeded! To the tune of thousands of dollars. The bad news? Let's hold up on that for a moment. First, let me tell you how the giant-killers beat the casinos.

Betting Biased Roulette Wheels:

Roulette wheels are created by craftsmen, but no man-made device is going to be flawless. Further, these wheels are sometimes subjected to abuse and inadequate maintenance once they leave the factory, increasing the chances for imperfections to develop—warpage, cracks, loosening of the metal slots between pockets, even rotational imbalances.

If any of these imperfections reach a point where they affect the outcome of play, then we may say the wheel is "biased." A "perfect" or "unbiased" wheel would be one where each number had an equal chance of coming up. An unbiased wheel is what the casino pays for. A biased wheel is what the gambler prays for! The reason? Any wheel imperfection that can alter results away from normal statistical expectations is a potential source of profit for the player.

Consider, for example, the single number bets on the layout. On the unbiased double-zero wheel, each number has an equal 1/38 chance of hitting. The casino pays off 35-1 on this bet (the proper odds would be 37-1, maintaining its 5.26% edge). Let us assume, however, that the wheel was biased in such a way that one number—say #9—came up more frequently than would be expected by chance, say about once every thirty spins. At that point anyone betting that number would, over the long run, have the percentages in their favor; they would, in effect, be playing an "unfair" game *against* the house.

How does a gambler find out if a wheel is biased to such a point that winning is possible? By "clocking" the wheel. This involves recording the results of a specified wheel over a *long* period of play, often a week or more. The results are then examined to see if any deviation

---

CLOCKING A ROULETTE WHEEL

The table on the following page is designed for recording all of the events that can come up on the American roulette wheel (which we have divided into six sections, for purposes of identification). At the end of several sessions at the same wheel, it should be apparent to you whether or not that wheel is biased. If you find that there has been any heavy concentration of action in any one section—or if there is a borderline concentration between two sections—you could suspect a bias. (This figure can also be used to test out systems: see "Beating Roulette Wheels by Physical Prediction," below.)

NUMBER CALLED															
SECTION 1																TOTAL ___
SECTION 2																TOTAL ___
SECTION 3																TOTAL ___
SECTION 4																TOTAL ___
SECTION 5																TOTAL ___
SECTION 6																TOTAL ___
RED																TOTAL ___
BLACK																TOTAL ___
ODD																TOTAL ___
EVEN																TOTAL ___
1st DOZEN																TOTAL ___
2nd DOZEN																TOTAL ___
3rd DOZEN																TOTAL ___
1–18 LOW																TOTAL ___
19–36 HIGH																TOTAL ___
1st COLUMN																TOTAL ___
2nd COLUMN																TOTAL ___
3rd COLUMN																TOTAL ___

from normal statistical expectations occur. It is only through patient, long-term observation of a wheel that one can determine if these deviations are occurring, and whether they are the result of chance fluctuations or of wheel imperfections.

Clocking the wheels is exactly what one man did in

order to win a fortune at the fabled Monte Carlo casino. His name was Jaggers, a skilled mechanic by trade, who dabbled in mathematics as a hobby. Jaggers was well aware that "imperfect man couldn't produce perfect machinery;" he was also aware of mathematical probabilities for roulette and what they meant in terms of winning and losing at the tables.

Putting this knowledge together, Jaggers saw a way to defeat Goliath. Going directly to Monte Carlo, he hired six clerks to clock six different roulette wheels. Day after day he poured over the clerks' figures, looking for any unusual patterns the wheels might be throwing. After five weeks of such painstaking clocking and analysis, he was ready to make his move. His strategy was to play those numbers that appeared more frequently than if they had merely been falling according to chance expectations.

When the smoke cleared, Jaggers left Monte Carlo with about sixty-five thousand pounds profit... not a bad payment for his labors! He could have gone on winning indefinitely, had the casino management not uncovered his tactics, then taken countermeasures.

The Jaggers success story has been duplicated by wheel-clockers in the United States and other parts of the world. Many of their exploits are detailed by Alan Wilson in his *Casino Gambler's Guide*, including the saga of the two American graduate students who went in search of biased wheels throughout Reno and Las Vegas, and came away with $30,000 in profits.

What about profit-taking from biased roulette wheels today? Can it be done? Can you do it? Several gambling experts say "no." Tom Ainslie (*How to Gamble in a Casino*) calls the search for biased wheels "a waste of time." Ian Anderson, the blackjack expert, agrees and points out that newer roulette wheels are "perfectly balanced." Then there is the bad news I mentioned earlier. If you do find a biased wheel, the chances of profit-taking will abruptly end if the casino discovers what you are doing. I already related how Jaggers was stopped by casino countermeasures; other gamblers have been similarly stopped when biased wheels were taken out of sevice by casino management.

But things aren't hopeless! I don't agree with those skeptics who see biased wheel coups as a thing of the past. With the rapid spread of casino gambling, the number of roulette wheels will increase in number. Further, maintenance problems and all the other potential conditions that favor the development of biased wheels will not go away—they will be with us as long as the "whirling ladies" continue to spin.

Casino management will be more aware of the biased wheel problem (as they are with blackjack counters), but that does not mean they will necessarily do much about it—unless they suspect that *their* wheels are biased.

Which brings me to this observation: most pit bosses become aware of biased wheels when players try to make a killing on them and do nothing to disguise their actions. This is foolish. The problem of casino detection is not insoluble. The player can, with proper camouflage, disguise his intentions and accomplish his coup. The need for a player to disguise activities at biased wheels is no different, really, than a card counter who must camouflage his skills at the blackjack tables.

If you have the time and patience you might find it interesting and worthwhile to pursue the biased wheel approach to giant-killing. Here are my recommendations for getting underway.

(1)   Read about the topic. Learn all you can. Find out how to clock the wheel properly. In addition to the chart included above, I recommend Wilson's *Casino*

Gambler's Guide, and Fisk's *The Gambler's Bible,* to get you on track (for information on these books, see Appendix A).

(2) Be sure to camouflage what you are doing, in both the clocking stage and playing stage. Make no mistake: if the casino management discovers that you are profiting from a biased wheel, they will change or repair that wheel.

(3) Be sure to clock it long enough so that you'll be able to determine whether an irregular pattern is the result of a biased wheel, or simply an unusual statistical deviation.

(4) If possible, look for single-zero biased wheels. The house percentage you will have to overcome is smaller.

(5) Check to see if there are published results of your wheel's performance. Many casinos provide these records for "systems" players. If this data is available, it will save you a lot of time and hassle.

Beating Roulette Wheels by "Physical" Prediction

A roulette wheel doesn't have to be biased to be beaten. There is another way, a very exciting and powerful way. Unfortunately, at its present stage of development, this "other way" is not yet available to the average player.

For many years now, individuals like Thorp and Wilson have surmised that it would be possible to beat roulette if, by using the laws of physics, one could determine where the roulette ball might land...in advance of its arrival. Wilson put it this way: "Today, when computers can predict complicated orbits and can guide a defensive

133

missile to intercept an attacking missile, it would appear to be child's play to predict where a roulette ball will land on the next spin. Provided one can assume reasonably consistent operation of the wheel, the mechanical situation is elementary. All you need are the 'initial conditions' at the instant the ball is spun, and some empirical data on the slowing down of the ball."[23]

Of course, the problem isn't all *that* simple. There are the various metal deflectors to contend with, and the unpredictable course of the ball as it hits the frets or bounces crazily out of the pockets. Yet, perfect prediction isn't needed. In fact, far from it. Simply being able to predict which *half* of the wheel the ball will plunk into would give the player such a whopping edge that he could "go for the chandeliers"...and make it!

The real problem with the physical prediction of roulette outcomes involves the development of equipment which could make such predictions possible *in casino play* while, at the same time, allow the player to camouflage what he is doing.

This involves the miniaturization of computers and other instruments to the extent that they could be concealed on a gambler's body. Should the casino ever realize what is afoot, they could simply require that all bets be placed *before* the ball is spun...totally negating the effectiveness of any physical prediction system.*

---

*Some students of roulette have argued that it is possible to make gross predictions about the sector in which a roulette ball will come to rest. They do this by analyzing the movements of the dealer—where he normally releases the ball, the speed of the ball, the speed of the wheel...all the factors under his control. Their goal is to find a dealer who is very stereotyped in his movements. Then, they argue, it might be possible to make predictions *before* the dealer releases the ball. I don't hold out very high hopes for such a method. . .but it is worthy of further study before anyone rejects it out of hand. (Just for the fun of it, you can run a little test yourself by using the chart for Clocking a Roulette Wheel, earlier this chapter.)

Looking like a science fiction scenario, there has already been an attempt made at physical prediction of roulette: two players fitted with hidden equipment took a shot at the casino coffers. They encountered some difficulties, yet their initial foray into the land of Goliath did indicate that there is a potential for future gain.

Dr. Thorp recently made a major statement concerning the physical prediction of roulette in a series of articles for *Gambling Times* Magazine. From the tenor of his works it seems obvious he, too, is confident that physical prediction of roulette can be achieved. It is interesting to note, in this regard, that when Thorp first proposed to publish his views, the editors of *Gambling Times* received a curious letter. It was an anonymous letter from a gambler who requested the material not be printed, lest it alert the casinos and endanger profits for players *already* making money from such an approach.

There is no way to determine whether the author(s) of the *Gambling Times* letter was, in fact, cashing in on the physical prediction of roulette. Yet it is my firm belief that such an approach to winning at roulette is entirely feasible; it probably already is a fact in certain instances, and will pose a threat to casino banks as long as the participants adequately disguise their play so as not to arouse suspicions and countermeasures from casino personnel.

For all you would-be "Davids" . . . I suggest you keep

abreast of exciting developments in this particular field
—it could mean significant profits at some later date.

Craps

Beat the dice tables? Ridiculous! Of all the casino
table games, craps seems the most immune to attack.
Yet, there are reports of "dice table Davids" successfully
assaulting the Casino-Goliath.

The most interesting coup is recounted in Andersen's
Turning the Tables on Las Vegas. He tells the story of a
don't pass bettor who also placed the 4 and 5, and made
a lot of *any craps* wagers. When he shot the dice, the
player always held them the same way: one atop the
other with both aces up. He released them the same way,
too—one die bouncing all over the table, the other skid-
ding and spinning about. Interestingly, the dice seemed
to show a disproportionate number of 1's (1,1; 1,2; 1,3;
1,4; etc.) That meant his totals were usually low (2, 3, 4,
5, 6)...and all were winning bets for this particular
shooter.

As Andersen looked on, the player took the casino for
$50,000 before they halted his play. It was only later
that Andersen got the real line on the "lucky" crap-
shooter. It turned out that he had spent ten years
perfecting a controlled dice shot on a crap table he had
purchased and set up in his home. Once he had his shot
under control...he took a shot at Vegas. The results (according to Andersen's sources): the sure-fingered player
racked up winnings in excess of *one million dollars.*

The idea that a shooter, after painstaking practice,
could control fair dice in a crap game is, of course, nothing
new. It has been done by dice sharps and "cross-roads"

players all over the country—*but not on regulation casino crap tables.* Supposedly, these regulation tables have been designed so as to make controlled throws impossible. Yet some don't quite come up to standard.

Gambling authority John Scarne describes an effective dice table controlled shot, in his comprehensive *Scarne on Dice.* He points out that such a shot "has taken many a casino operator for a bundle..." and that once his book "hits the stands, dice-table manufacturers will make certain that it can't work on their tables." Obviously, some of them haven't taken Scarne's advice.[24]

What about you? How can you win at craps? Well, one way is to buy a crap table, practice for a decade, and come out smokin' (presumably on a crap table with a flaw like the one described by Scarne). Another way might be to watch for any other gambler who seems to shoot the dice in a systematic manner...consistently achieving results that don't seem to jibe with statistical expectations. Then: bet the way the shooter does! Of course, before you would want to bet with the shooter you would want to see if he is a winner—many dice players who couldn't control a dice shot if their lives depended on it, pick up and throw the dice in a specific way due to superstitious beliefs.

It is my hunch that, in the coming years, more and more players will experiment with controlled dice shots... and some of them will be successful. Remember, with the extremely low house advantage in craps, a player would only have to be minimally successful in controlling the dice to rack up a favorable statistical edge.

If you should be one of those shooters who *is* able to develop a controlled shot—a vital word of advice. Camouflage, once again, is of the essence if you have any intention of continuing your shooting ways. Pit bosses are quick learners. Once they're stung by an obvious controlled shot, they won't let it happen again. Don't *you* be obvious. Limit your winnings per session. Don't shoot too long in any one place. Don't take a controlled shot every time—mix it in with other "normal shots" to divert suspicion. Most of all, don't act like the cat that is about to swallow the mouse. If you truly are good enough to beat the casino with a controlled shot—don't puff up your chest, tell your friends, or boast to the dealers. Get rich in the dark—you'll last longer. Remember, you can't win if you can't play.

Finally, don't delude yourself into thinking you have mastered a controlled shot when you haven't. Some gamblers will use any excuse possible to get down a bet they shouldn't be making. Don't think you can beat the dice tables unless you really can—and have proved it in actual play, making *small bets* until your skill is established beyond doubt. The gentleman in Andersen's book practiced for *ten years* before he laid down a bet. That might be a good thing to keep in mind the next time you take on Goliath at the crap tables.

The Shape of Things to Come

There is no reason to believe that the players' assault on the casino will slow. Gamblers are a clever lot—always looking for an angle to render the casinos broke. The casino owners aren't dumb, either. They know they must keep their guard up—be ready to meet any challenges players may make against their profits.

What we have, then, is a game of cat and mouse . . . an undeclared war . . . with both sides probing for an advantage, a way to gain the edge. The player must realize, when he goes into battle, that the odds are stacked against him. This comes about by the very nature of the war which is fought on the casino turf, with the initial rules and percentages favoring the house. On top of that, there are the powerful Vegas ploys designed to psych out the gambler and keep the possibility of success remote from him.

The player's only hope is to turn the tables on the house, to psych out Vegas and find a way to overcome the house edge—and do it in a way that the house hasn't anticipated and/or won't detect.

In the near future, the clash between casino player and owner should become even more interesting. New scientific interest in gambling, plus technical progress in computers and electronics, literally guarantees exciting new developments. Each of you, as members of the gambling public, should keep on top of these developments—be alert for pieces of information that might get you an edge during play. You might even take a professor to dinner. If his name is Edward Thorp.

CHAPTER 11

HOW TO WIN...
AND NOT GET BARRED

"Las Vegas loves visitors—
but many casinos don't love
winners. They will, on occa-
sion, ask you to leave. Not for
doing anything wrong.
Nothing shady ...Just plain
winning. A cardinal sin. And
one worthy of excommunica-
tion. Exclusion. Remember
now, I'm not talking about
blackjack counters...I'm
talking about honest, albeit
lucky, players. I'm talking
about winners."

—*Lyle Stuart*
Casino Gambling for the
Winner

> "You can't win if you can't
> play."
> —*A Gambler's Lament*

I want to tell you a Vegas story that is so incredible you probably wouldn't believe it if I retold it in my own words. So I'm going to quote it directly from the source, Mike Goodman, who describes the incident in his book, *Your Best Bet*.

"A stickman at the crap table called a twenty minute hand and the club lost quite a few thousand to the hand. The stickman got off the table and started to cough. A boss who was rough on the help was watching the dice passing. He said to the dealer, 'What's the matter?'

The dealer said, 'My throat hurts.'

The boss said, 'Here is a remedy for your cough.' He took a penknife out of his pocket, gave it to the dealer. Said, 'When you get home, use this and cut your throat.'

The dealer quit that night."[25]

Goodman tells other stories of casino managers who hated to see gamblers win, including one boss who kicked blackjack dealers in the shins if they lost with a busted hand. It got so bad, the dealers had to buy shin guards to protect their legs![26] Although these stories are unusual, they do serve to make a point: *casino management doesn't cotton to players who consistently win house money*. And, if bosses are willing to kick losing *dealers* in the shins, imagine what might be in store for winning *players*. I have read and been told some pretty incredible tales in this regard, including one incident where a player was supposedly barred from casino play and driven to the airport...in the trunk of a car. Other players have claimed they were roughed up by casino security forces. Again, these stories are also unusual, but they do serve to reemphasize a legitimate concern of all gamblers: winning can be an expensive proposition in Las Vegas.

Many people find it difficult to believe that Vegas doesn't love winners. As I pointed out earlier, casino owners love the *publicity* that winners generate...but don't let that fool you. The occasional winner is touted— but the *steady* winner is a target for scorn and even casino expulsion. Don't take my word for it: ask any competent blackjack counter...if you can find one that hasn't been barred from casino play.

Actually, when you stop to consider that gambling is a business which profits from players' losses, then the behavior of casino management becomes more understandable. Every business takes steps to survive and prosper, and the gambling business is no exception. There can be only one steady winner in a gambling town and, from the Vegas point of view, it had better not be the player!

Harassment of Winning Players

Most people who gamble in Vegas will never incur the wrath of the casinos because the vast majority of gamblers will lose. Occasional winners will escape hassles as well. They pose no serious threat to the casino bank and, besides, sporadic winners are good for business. But what about players like yourself—individuals who gamble smart, manage money wisely, and know how to psych out Vegas? In other words, what about the *steady* winner? I sincerely doubt you will find yourself in the trunk of an automobile on the way to the airport; yet, some form of casino harassment is certainly a possibility.

There are many ways casino management can hassle you to make your life—and winning—more difficult. Minor harassment takes the form of *dealing irritants*—procedures whereby casino personnel make table play more unpleasant and unprofitable for the gambler. Here are some examples:

(1)   As you win steadily, your once-friendly dealer becomes increasingly ill-tempered and rude.

(2)   Games are slowed down or sped up to interfere with your concentration and enjoyment at the tables. Oftentimes, dealers are switched in and out of your game at irregular intervals to further complicate play.

(3)   Pit bosses and other floor personnel stand close by, scrutinizing your action with grim eyes and a sullen demeanor. The more you win, the more sullen they become.

(4)   Your requests for various services are granted grudgingly, or ignored altogether.

(5)   In blackjack, the dealer frequently shuffles the cards . . . sometimes every few hands, or immediately after you raise your bet significantly.*

---

*According to blackjack player and author Stanley Roberts, one Las Vegas casino gave its blackjack dealers the following instructions:

"The following rules must be memorized, learned and

applied. Failure to comply will result in three (3) days off for the first offense and termination upon the second offense.

(1) Shuffle any time a total of six 4's, 5's, and 6's have been placed in the discard rack (used up).

(2) Shuffle any time a player raises his bet to four times his minimum bet in that deck.

(3) Shuffle any time a new player arrives at your table, when hands have been played, and the wager is $20 or more.

(4) Shuffle when instructed to do so by the pitboss."[27]

Minor harassment is often enough to discourage a player from gaining the winning edge. Used in conjunction with the fabulous treatment afforded to losers, the casino has a potent combination punch for psyching out the gambler. Most players like to have fun and want to feel liked when they gamble. The casinos make sure players do. . .when they lose. When they win steadily, however, players are made to feel unpopular, out of place . . .almost unpatriotic. Kind of like a New Yorker fan rooting for the Yankees against Boston in the middle of Fenway Park.

Some gamblers can handle this type of harassment and rejection. They aren't home free, however, because the casino can still bring its ultimate harassment weapon into play: "barring" a player from their premises. The winning player is simply kicked out of the casino. And, unless the courts force the casinos to readmit these individuals, that is that.

It used to be that such "barring" was a rarity. This has all changed, however, as increasing numbers of players are mounting sustained assaults on casino banks. Now casino management is quite willing to ask gamblers to leave their premises, if it looks like a player might be a steady winner.

The most likely place for a player to encounter harassment and possible expulsion is at the blackjack tables—where the greatest potential for beating the house exists. But such tactics can be encountered at any casino game where a gambler is a consistent winner. This is because the "blackjack scare" has made some casino officials suspicious to the point of paranoia where winning players are concerned. Thus, they often overreact to gamblers who make a reasonable run at house money . . . even though their success might be entirely due to "luck," and have nothing whatsoever to do with skillful play.

A classic example of this casino management paranoia is revealed in the following interview with a gaming executive:

"... I asked a casino manager what he would do if a player, without cheating, consistently won at craps. His answer was prompt and curt: 'I'd throw him out!' 'But if you knew everything was on the square,' I pressed, 'wouldn't you think the odds would eventually catch up with him?' 'Look,' he said, 'I don't care if the guy has a halo around his head and constantly recites *Hail Marys*—if he wins regularly, he's out! It's not our business to figure out how a guy is winning. We're not in business to support winners while we figure out how they're doing it. If we don't like their action, that's it!' "[28]

What can you do to protect yourself against possible harassment? Basically, there are two viable approaches. You can stop winning, or you can start camouflaging your winning. I fervently hope you utilize the second approach! Camouflaging your winning casino play isn't all that difficult; in fact, if you have any leaning toward the thespian, it can be downright enjoyable.

Camouflage: Your Defense Against Harassment

Ian Andersen is a rarity in Las Vegas. He is a player who wins *steadily* at the blackjack tables year after year, but never gets harassed. In fact, he is welcomed as a valued guest by the major Vegas casinos which wine and dine him while he takes them for a bundle! How does he do it? By camouflaging his winning ways.

Andersen learned something very important in his early gambling days: you can't win if you can't play. After being thrown out of several casinos for being too successful, he began to realize that winning involved more than counting cards and managing money properly. So he developed a blueprint for psyching out Vegas—a strategy that avoided harassment through the skillful use of camouflage while gambling. He presents this strategy in his delightful book, *Turning the Tables on Las Vegas*. I heartily recommend the text for all casino gamblers, because what Andersen reveals about camouflage can be applied to all table games, not just blackjack.

What are some of the camouflaging techniques you can utilize to avoid (or minimize) casino harassment while you win at the tables? From my own experiences, plus suggestions from literature on gambling, let me recommend the following:

The Hit and Run

No, this is not a traffic offense or a baseball tactic. The "hit and run" is a strategy for camouflaging winning by keeping each gambling session short, no longer than an hour in length. Playing this way makes it difficult for the casino personnel to "get a handle" on your gambling skills and winning capabilities. No sooner does the pit boss begin paying attention to your play when—snap!— you're finished and you're on your way out the door.

Even if you win handsomely in the sixty minute session, casino management will be hard pressed to determine whether it was a result of luck or skill. After all, lots of players get lucky for an hour. It is only when a gambler wins steadily—consistently—that casino personnel become suspicious and consider countermeasures. Sixty minutes just isn't enough time to check out your play, determine if you are a long-term threat, and institute action against you.

Dr. Thorp refers to this "hit and run" strategy as the "paper route" approach. It is aptly named. What you are basically doing is going to casinos door-to-door, collecting from your "customers" as you walk your route. There are three important things you must do in establishing an effective hit and run strategy:

(1) Keep playing sessions short...an hour is ideal (some experts recommend even shorter periods of time, around forty-five minutes).

(2) If you begin winning big from the outset of a session and you feel casino personnel are getting suspicious of your play...don't hesitate to cut that playing session short.

(3) Once you complete a session, don't play again until you are in a different casino. (If you play at two different tables in the same establishment, the casino management will have twice as long to observe your play. This gives them more information and increases your chances of being harassed should you

win.)

The Round Robin

The "round robin" should be used in conjunction with the hit and run strategy just presented. In sports, a "round robin" refers to a tournament where each participant is matched against every other participant. In gambling, we also have a "tournament": you against the various casinos. Your goal should be to play "round robin" style, moving from casino to casino...never playing at the same casino twice until you've played at every different casino once. The reason for this strategy, as with the hit and run approach, is to keep your winning ability hidden and your face relatively unknown.

There are dozens of casinos in Las Vegas. There are also three shifts of casino personnel in each one. This means that, using the round robin style, you could play approximately once a day for three months yet never encounter the same casino personnel across the tables. Now I ask you: what pit boss is going to remember a gambler he sees every few months...or every few weeks, for that matter? Particularly when that gambler stays at the tables for less than an hour per session.

Most gamblers risk harassment if they win steadily at one casino over a relatively long period of constant play. You dramatically reduce the odds of this ever happening to you when you spread your wins around many casinos, and keep those wins confined to periods of short play, say, sixty minutes or less.

Now...what happens if you don't complete a full round robin before playing in the same casino twice? Let's say, for instance, that you decide to avoid a few

establishments because they make you feel uncomfortable when you play. Or maybe you skip over a few
casinos that are across town and too difficult to reach.
Then, too, there are some casinos that enforce gambling
rules unfavorable to the player (see Chapter 12). There's
no question you'll steer clear of such places, avoiding
them like the plague.

*Don't worry: it is not necessary to play in every Las
Vegas casino to make a round robin effective.* It is the
spirit, rather than the letter of the round robin law, that
is important. Thus, you should play in *enough* different
casinos to keep your consistent winning pattern disguised.
Obviously, how many casinos constitute "enough"
depends on how often you play...and how often you
win. If you play every day and win frequently, you'll
want to gamble in a greater number of different casinos
than the individual who comes to Vegas to gamble five
weekends a year. Use your judgment here. Again, your
goal is to keep a low profile. Playing in different gambling establishments will help you achieve that goal.

Keeping a Gambler's Log

One advantage to playing in different casinos is you'll
be able to discover which ones have the most favorable
rules and playing conditions for the gambler. Once you
know this information you can limit your gambling to
those establishments which give you the best chance of
winning.

Every serious gambler should keep a casino log or
"diary." It can be an invaluable aid in a comprehensive
winning strategy. After each gambling session, all of the
following information should be recorded in your log (See
Figure #1). Fill in the data *after* you leave the casino.

(1) Date of the session
(2) Locations of the session
(3) Game played
(4) Time the session started and ended
(5) Gambling stake for the session
(6) Starting bet
(7) Betting range (smallest and largest bet for the session)
(8) Average bet size
(9) Amount won (+) or lost (–) for the session
(10) Observations: Unusual event that took place at the session and/or information that would help or hinder winning in future sessions (e.g., harassment by casino personnel, rule changes, etc).

FIGURE 1: A Typical Gambler's Log Entry

DATE: 1/9/82
CASINO: MGM Grand, Las Vegas
GAME: Blackjack
TIME IN: 2:15 p.m. TIME OUT: 3:05 p.m. TOTAL: 50 Minutes
STAKE: $500
STARTING BET: $15
SMALLEST BET: $10 LARGEST BET: $25
AVERAGE BET SIZE: $20
AMOUNT WON/LOST: $45 (+)

OBSERVATIONS: Dealer, Bill, quiet but not hostile. No pressure from the pit. Table crowded up near end of session. No early shuffle-ups.

No dealer "tells" spotted.

A Typical Gambler's Log Entry

This information can then be used in planning your subsequent gambling activities. Without a diary, it is often difficult to remember when and how often you gambled at a certain casino, making round robin scheduling difficult. Also, people have a tendency to forget which gaming establishments are most favorable for the player. The more you play...the more likely these memory lapses become. This is because the various sessions blend together, making individual events difficult to pinpoint.

After you have kept a log over a significant period of time (a year or longer), the information it can provide becomes particularly useful. For instance, you can go back over the sessions and see if any winning and/or losing patterns are developing at certain playing times, or in certain casinos, or even at different betting levels. Many gamblers have been able to improve their winning percentages in just this way.

One of my friends kept a log and discovered that he lost more frequently during morning playing sessions. He had no explanation for this, although he suspected it might be due to his inability to concentrate early in the day. At any rate, he cut out playing before noon and his win rate subsequently increased.

Another gambler told me that keeping a log helped him discover a significant losing pattern at one particular casino. As a result, he stopped playing at that establishment, and his winnings increased. Some players I know keep a list of casinos they will not enter...a kind of gamer's answer to the casino "Brown Book," published by the Griffin Detective Agency, which contains photographs of gamblers barred from the tables in Las Vegas.

Watching the Range of Your Bets

Casino personnel get very suspicious when players make significant changes in the size of their bets. At the blackjack tables, for example, some dealers will automatically "shuffle up" if a gambler makes a bet four or more times larger than his typical wager.

It is often better to keep the size of your bets in a "safe" range and win more slowly, than to try for a big killing and risk the danger of casino harassment.

Handling Wins and Losses

If you are losing during a particular session, don't be afraid to converse with casino personnel about your "bad luck." It never hurts to have a loss observed by casino management. On the other hand, if you are winning, play down your success. Learning how to deftly slip chips into your pocket helps immensely. Nothing arouses casino interest more quickly than a player surrounded by a steadily growing stack of chips.

Learning to Act Like a Typical Vegas Loser

Here's where the thespian aspect of camouflage comes into play. You want to look and act like a gambler who's going to lose, not someone who's going to take the casino for a bundle. You've got to psych the casino management into thinking you've succumbed to their temptations. If you're successful at playing the role of the typical Vegas loser, the chances of encountering harassment from the casino will be small. Here are a few "act-ing" recommendations:

(1) Act like you're out for a good time. Display an "it's-only-money" attitude.

(2) Don't play like a cold, human computer; gamble with flesh and blood enthusiasm.

(3) Don't act guilty, as if you're doing something illegal. Interact with casino personnel, don't try to avoid them. Be relaxed, not uptight.

(4) Look like a typical Vegas visitor, not a professional card hustler.[29]

Be a Gambling Chameleon

A chameleon is a tenacious little creature that survives by using camouflage. The next time you're ready for an assault on the casino bank take a moment to think about the chameleon. And then practice the camouflage that will help you survive at the tables. It's another way to psych out Vegas...and win.

The Casino Dealer: Friend or Foe?

What do most gamblers see when they look across the green felt? The enemy. After all, the dealer is hired to protect the casino bank...the very thing the player is trying to capture. But: does the dealer have to be an enemy? In fact, wouldn't it be better if you could make the dealer an ally rather than an adversary at the tables?

Why Should I Try to Get the Dealer on My Side?

Let me assure you that establishing a cooperative, rather than an adversarial, relationship with a casino dealer is one of the most important things you can do to win. . . and not get barred from casino action. Yet, many gamblers don't understand why this is so. "Why should I try to get the dealer on my side?" they want to know, ". . . especially in games like roulette and craps where the dealer has no influence over what happens."

The truth of the matter is: either directly or indirectly, *the dealer can influence your winning and losing in all casino games*. This is particularly so in blackjack (see pp. 152–156) but it also holds true, to varying degrees, throughout the gaming establishment. If a dealer doesn't like you, here are just a few of the things that could happen.

(1) A dealer can intimidate you and/or make your stay at the tables unpleasant. This tactic, more than any other, can play havoc with a player's bankroll and lead to monstrous losses at the casino. Many players, when confronted with a hostile, intimidating casino employee, become unnerved—psyched out—and gamble less effectively. They don't enjoy the gaming experience and they pay dearly for it at the same time. Now that's a double loss in any player's book.

(2) Your requests for information and service will be ignored whenever possible. It is amazing how difficult it is to get the attention of a dealer (or order a drink) once that employee wants to ignore you.

(3) In any dispute, a dealer can side "with the house," making it more difficult for you to win even a legitimate complaint.

155

(4)   You can be "cheated." I put the word in quotes because the cheating of disliked players is a unique kind of dishonesty which can be totally avoided by the gambler who behaves decently at the tables. As I pointed out elsewhere, the vast majority of dealers are honest, hardworking employees doing their best at a trying, often frustrating, job. When they resort to "cheating" a disliked player, it isn't for personal profit or to help the casino; it is a last resort they use to get rid of the customer, and to retaliate against treatment they view as unfair or unjustified. Frankly, in the few instances I have witnessed dealers cheating obnoxious customers, it has been richly deserved.

Dealers "cheating" against disliked players is relatively rare, partially due to casino scrutiny and partly because most dealers don't like to do it except in the most pressing circumstances. When it does occur, it normally takes these forms: (A) manipulation of the gaming equipment in an illegal manner (i.e., dealing seconds from a deck of cards); (B) shortchanging the player during bet payoffs. This can be accomplished much more easily than you might imagine. Most gamblers don't count their payoffs; they just assume the amount is accurate. A chip or two missing every so often is easily overlooked. Think about your own behavior. How often do you check each payoff as it comes from the dealer? In the heat of play, particularly during winning streaks, or at the crap table where multiple bets and variable payoffs occur at a rapid clip, I hardly know of any gamblers who count their payoffs each time they are received. And when a player is excited, tired and/or a bit tipsy—which is all too often—the opportunity for successfully shortchanging him is dramatically increased.

Now, then, what happens if a dealer *does* like you?

Nice things...like the creation of a psychological climate conducive to gambling fun and profit. Here is how a dealer can help you at the tables:

(1) He can increase your profit margin. As in the case of "cheating" just discussed, this type of dealer help is not usually motivated by desire for personal profit* or to hurt the casino. It is a kind of "thank you" for exemplary player behavior at the tables. This kind of dealer activity cannot be conducted with impunity due to casino scrutiny; thus, it is relatively rare. When it does occur, it usually involves overpaying on winning bets and/or "tipping off" cards (in blackjack).

(2) He can ignore call bets or declare them "no bet" when those wagers are losers on the table. A case in point: I was playing in a fast action, crowded crap game. The shooter was in the middle of a long roll. Just before he tossed the dice I made a call bet, "Sixty dollars each on the 6 and 8." Before I could put the chips on the layout, the shooter tossed the dice and sevened-out. "Here," I said, taking five $25 chips from the rail. "Keep it," said the boxman, "it was no bet."

(3) A dealer can aid your play by reminding you of certain bets or payoffs you might otherwise have overlooked.

(4) In a dispute, a dealer can side with you, making it easier for you to win any complaint against the house.

(5) Your requests for information and service will receive immediate attention.

---

*Except when performed for "tokes" (to be discussed on p.154), or a part of a player-dealer team activity, purposely aimed at trying to "rip off" the casino.

(6) The dealer will be congenial and help make your gambling more relaxed and enjoyable. Just as an intimidating dealer can unnerve a player and reduce his gambling effectiveness, so can a friendly dealer psychologically support a player and enhance his gambling effectiveness at the tables.

The Special Case of "21"

It is always to your advantage to get the dealer "on your side" when it comes to gambling in a casino; but in the case of blackjack, it is absolutely essential. In "21," if a dealer doesn't like you, he can shut you down...pure and simple. And he doesn't have to "cheat" to do it. All he has to do is constantly shuffle-up or, worse, tell the pit boss he suspects you of counting. Your playing days at that casino will be over, period. On the other hand, if a blackjack dealer likes you he can increase your profit potential by dealing the deck down, shuffling away ten-poor decks, flashing the burn card, etc. (assuming he can do so without attracting the wrath of casino management). Ian Andersen was totally correct when he referred to the blackjack dealer as a "$20,000 a year gift." Such a person can be worth that much to you...sometimes even more. There is no other casino game where the dealer's attitude toward the player can mean so much in terms of cold, hard cash. The next time you sit down at a blackjack table and eye the dealer across the green felt, keep his importance in mind. That's one person you want on your side, rooting *for* you rather than *against* you!

How Can I Get the Dealer "On My Side"?

To answer this question, I want you to think back to the beginning of this chapter. . . to the stories about the dealers who were abused by their casino bosses when they dealt winning hands to various players. Now, it is true that most dealers won't be kicked in the shins or given penknives to commit suicide if gamblers get hot at their tables; yet, it is also true that dealers *are* under constant pressure by casino management to make sure the house wins (particularly in blackjack where the house knows the game can be beaten by competent players). To make matters worse, most gamblers expect to win, too. . . and they put pressure on the dealers when they don't. Which leaves the dealer between a rock and a hard place: if he wins too often he's hassled by irate players, and if he doesn't win enough he's criticized by casino management.

Put yourself in the dealer's place. How would *you* like to work under such circumstances? Throw in long work days and lack of employment security, and you have one hell of a job! I venture to say if the average gambler were suddenly thrust into the role of dealer he would come away from the experience with a healthy respect for the men and women behind the tables.

Which brings us back to the question: "How can you get the dealer on your side?" The answer is to treat him the way you'd want to be treated. Remember, a casino dealer is no different than any other human being. . . he needs, he aches, he loves, he hates—just like you and me. If you treat him with kindness he will respond accordingly. The problem is—as I mentioned earlier—most players don't see the dealer as someone to treat with kindness. . . they see him as "THE ENEMY". . . the foe. . . someone to DEFEAT.

The problem with viewing the dealer as an enemy is

that you treat him like one. This, in turn, causes the dealer to treat you in a similar fashion. It is a vicious circle . . . and an unpleasant one, for the dealer and player alike.

What I am going to ask you to do is pull off a "psych-out" of the first magnitude—I want you to psych the dealer into becoming your ally. *I want you to establish a partnership, not a contest, between you and the dealer.*[30] If you can't stop thinking of the dealer as an enemy, then go ahead and think it—*but DON'T treat him like one.* Instead, behave in the following manner at the tables.

(1) Be friendly and courteous to casino personnel. Most dealers are accustomed to abuse and rude behavior by players who see them as the enemy; thus, they appreciate gamblers who treat them with kindness and respect.

(2) Don't act like you are better than the dealer. This is not an ego-contest you're involved in. It is an activity where you are trying to win some money.

(3) When you are winning, "toke" the dealer. Think of the tip as an investment, an investment in dealer goodwill. This is particularly important in black-jack, where a dealer can literally "shut a counter down." It is not necessary to *overtip* in order to gain dealer goodwill. You should tip in proportion to your bet size and winnings—*not* to impress the dealer or to give away your hard-earned profits in outlandish tokes. Remember, you're bucking some pretty rough percentages when you sit down at the tables. The dealers realize this, and don't expect you to give them everything you win.

When you do tip, make it in the form of a bet for the dealer. (For instance: in craps, if you're betting the pass line, make a pass line bet for the "boys." In blackjack: when you make your wager, make one for the dealer, too. Do so *before* the cards are dealt. That way, if you win, so does he.) This kind of tipping will help underscore your partner relationship with the dealer, the idea that you both need each other for a winning session.

(4) Don't be afraid to play against a dealer of the opposite sex. When you do, be friendly and cheerful ...it helps brighten up a dealer's otherwise dull routine. Some players feel that a bit of tasteful flirtation can sometimes work wonders for making a dealer more responsive to their needs as a person *and* a player. Dealers differ in their attitudes (and reactions) toward such flirtations, however, and should you engage in any, make sure they are in good taste. Of course, if your flirtations are not appreciated by the dealer, stop them at once.

(5) Strike up a conversation with the dealer, if you can do so comfortably, and will not be distracted from play. Not all dealers like to speak with customers but many appreciate the opportunity to move beyond the mechanical level of player-dealer interaction.

(6) When a dealer does a good job at the tables, it never hurts to praise him for his efforts. I make it a point to compliment a dealer whenever I feel he has provided me with good service. I think he deserves the praise—and it makes him feel better about me and his job.

(7) When you establish good rapport with a specific dealer, be sure to note his name and employing casino in your logbook. That way you will be able to identify and target him for additional play in the future.

(8) Not everybody is going to like you...no matter
    how hard you try. If you're playing against a dealer
    who remains hostile despite your best efforts...
    move to another table or, better still, to another
    casino. There are thousands of dealers in Las Vegas;
    don't get stuck with one who wants to see you lose.

* * *

It is a problem to be a consistent winner yet not get
barred from casino action. But it is a problem that can be
overcome with the skillful use of camouflage and the
proper interaction with casino personnel. The next time
you sit down to play, view the dealer across the table as
your friend, not your foe. Be congenial and treat that
person with respect. If you do, you'll feel better as a person, and you'll be psyching out Vegas at the same time.

CHAPTER 12

HOW TO CHOOSE AND USE A CASINO

> "When I buy a car I shop
> around for the best deal, so
> why should it be any different
> when I gamble? An amateur
> might think all casinos are the
> same, but they're not. I com-
> parison shop and choose the
> establishment that gives me
> the best odds for my money."
> —Las Vegas Gambler

If you believe that competition is healthy for American
business, then you're going to love Las Vegas. Unlike
some gambling spots, Vegas is not a one-casino town—
there are literally dozens of gaming establishments, all
vying for *your* business. This creates a situation where
casinos must "hustle" to attract customers; after all, if

one casino doesn't offer the player suitable incentives, there's another establishment that will, just down the street.

Discriminating gamblers take advantage of this "buyer's market," and they comparison shop among the various casinos for "bargains." Then they gamble at those establishments which offer the most advantageous playing conditions.

You'll want to use this comparison shopping approach when you gamble in Las Vegas, and I'll be providing a shopping "checklist" to aid you in your casino selection. First, though, I want you to consider . . .

The Primary Reason for Selecting a Casino

When it comes to choosing a gambling establishment, ask yourself this "bottom line" question:

Which casino offers me the best chance of winning?

When you find the answer to that question, you'll know where you should be gambling in Las Vegas.

In my own experience, I have discovered four factors which are important in determining a casino's "favorableness" for the player.

The first factor centers on *the rules for conducting the various games*. Some casinos play by rules that increase the house's advantage over the player. These are the casinos you'll want to avoid. Other establishments, however, play by rules that are more advantageous to the gambler—for example, some may permit double odds bets at craps or allow doubling down on any two cards in blackjack.

The second factor involves *the payouts on various bets*. Casinos are not obligated to make identical payoffs on various table bets, even when the wagers are the same. And they don't. Some establishments are more "liberal" in the payouts to their customers—returning a higher percentage of the monies wagered. This is true for slot machines, keno, and most table games. In craps, for instance, English casinos give better odds on certain bets than their American counterparts. Similarly, downtown Vegas casinos are generally more "liberal" than those on the Strip.

The third factor focuses on *the degree to which the casino hassles winners*. Some establishments are more tolerant toward players who consistently beat the house. These casinos are certainly worth locating...and using.

The fourth factor is more difficult to define, but it is definitely a part of every casino. I am referring to *the psychological atmosphere* created by the gambling establishment. This atmosphere is created by the individual (or corporate) casino owners, and reflects their particular attitudes and policies concerning the way a gaming establishment should be run. This atmosphere, in turn, affects the play of individual gamblers, each with his own attitudes and playing policies at the tables. Sometimes the atmosphere increases a gambler's winning potential; other times it hinders chances for success. It all depends on whether the particular casino atmosphere makes the player feel comfortable or disturbed at the tables...whether it psychs him out or helps him out.

Because each gambler is unique, there is no one best casino atmosphere for *every* player. An establishment that presents a good winning atmosphere for one individual might have quite the opposite impact on the person standing next to him at the tables.

It becomes imperative then that a favorable match be

achieved between the psychological atmosphere of the individual casino and the personality characteristics of the individual gambler. The only way you can attain such a match is to play in the various casinos and see which ones feel "right."

In my own gambling experiences, I have encountered very definite feelings of harmony or tension, depending on whether the casino I was in matched or clashed with my particular personality needs. The psychological atmosphere of Caesars Palace is very much in tune with my particular psychological needs. It helps me win. On the other hand, I feel uncomfortable when I'm gaming at the Hilton. The Hilton is a great place to play...the atmosphere just isn't right for me. So I don't play there anymore. For someone else, the results might be reversed...they might feel ill at ease in the "Palace" but totally relaxed at the Hilton.

Again, the important thing is to find a casino atmosphere that's right for you. That's what counts.

Your "Casino Locator" Checklist

Choosing a casino that's right for *you* is a highly personal matter. It involves feelings that are hard to define in scientific terms; attitudes that are difficult to express in words. Nevertheless, there are some casino characteristics you'll want to consider in selecting the gambling establishments that are best for you.

When I go on a "casino selection" mission, I bring along a *casino locator checklist* to make my task easier (See Figure #2). The items on the checklist correspond to the four factors I have already identified as important in determining a casino's "favorableness" for the player. Here are a few suggestions to help you "rate" the various casinos with your casino locator checklist.

(1)   Upon entering a casino, focus your attention on the game(s) you intend to play. Fill out a separate checklist for each game you are interested in playing. This is important—as the playing atmosphere and favorability of the different gambling activities can vary within the same casino.

(2)   Study the *rules* for the game(s) in question. Make a mental note of what they are. Later on you will want to write them down on your checklist for comparison with the rules in other casinos. This way you will be able to locate the casino(s) that offers rules most favorable for the players.

(3)   Study the *payoffs* on the various wagers for the game(s) you intend to play. Again, make a mental note on the payoff odds so you can compare them with those offered at other gambling establishments. Once you become familiar with the *rules* and *payoffs* at several casinos, it will be relatively easy to pick out gambling "bargains" (rules and/or payoffs that afford the gambler a greater opportunity for winning). This is because such bargains "stand out"—just like a good price for gasoline will be readily apparent to the comparison shopper.

(4)   Observe the interaction between the players and the casino personnel. Is it friendly and relaxed? Are the dealers courteous and helpful? What about winners —how are they treated? Are they harassed? If you're lucky, you might be able to observe a steady winner in action and note the reaction of casino management toward him.

(5)   Walk around the casino and get a feeling for its playing atmosphere. Do you feel comfortable? Tense? Confident? Insecure? Would you want to

play at the tables? Is it too noisy? What about the decor? Is the casino too large or small? How do you think you'd do? What you are trying to do is get a feel for the casino's *psychological atmosphere* to see if it fits with your personality needs. You might not be able to make a final decision without having a go at the tables. If this is the case . . . go ahead and play —assuming the other points on your casino locator checklist indicate that this casino is "good" for the player.

(6)   Once you have made your mental notes on points 2-5 delineated above, leave the casino and fill out your casino locator checklist. Do it right away, while your memory is still fresh—that way your checklist will be more accurate and complete.

(7)   Update your casino locator checklists at regular intervals. Gambling establishments, like other businesses, can change from time to time—particularly when there are shakeups in top management. It is possible for a favorable casino to become unfavorable, and vice-versa, as the rules, payoffs, employee attitudes and psychological atmosphere evolve in a particular establishment.

FIGURE 2-1

A Typical Casino Locator Checklist
NOTE: That the emphasis is on identifying favorable and unfavorable conditions that differentiate the casino under examination from other gambling establishments. Note also, that judgments on "interaction" and "atmosphere" are specific to the individual rater's needs, and will vary from player to player (some gamblers, for example, will *like* the large size of the MGM casino and crap tables).

DATE: 1/9/82

CASINO: MGM, Vegas

GAME: Craps

RULES:	Single odds only Good betting range ($5.00-$2,000) Come, place, buy bets allowed Finger bets allowed

----

PAYOFFS:	Standard on pass, come, buy, place Proposition bets payoff lower than in some casinos (e.g., Reno)

INTERACTION:	Relatively reserved...polite but not enthusiastic (might be result of table size, see below).

ATMOSPHERE:	Casino too large. Crap tables huge—destroys sense of intimacy, increases sense of impersonality. Definitely not a "homey" casino like Sands. Area around tables noisy when people line up for shows—somewhat distracting. Good ventilation.

After you have visited several casinos, you will be in a position to compare them, *vis-a-vis* "favorableness" to the player. Once that is accomplished you'll be able to gamble in those establishments that offer *you* the best chance of winning.

Using Your Gambler's "Log" to Identify Favorable Casinos

The "Casino Locator Checklist" is one way to identify "good" places to gamble. Another way involves the use of your "Gambler's Log" (See Figure #1, p. 151). After you have kept a log for a significant period of time, it can reveal some valuable information about those casinos in which you should gamble.

To get this information you will have to go back over your past gambling sessions and see if any winning or losing patterns have been established in certain casinos. Recall the gambler who did exactly that, then discovered a significant losing pattern at a particular casino. He stopped playing in that establishment and his winning increased.

If you've been keeping a log, it certainly will be worth your while to check for any win or loss patterns by casino. It will give you an *empirical read-out of your perform- ance, and figures don't lie.* I mention this because some players tend to distort their win-loss records in casinos they like . . . remembering their wins and forgetting the times that they got beaten. This can be a costly mistake if the gambler's mental distortion of the facts is extreme. Play it safe . . . keep an accurate log, and check it every once in a while for your casino-by-casino performance.

Choosing a Casino and Using the "Round Robin" Technique

In Chapter 11, I discussed the round robin method for avoiding casino harassment. It involved going from casino to casino...never playing at the same establishment twice, until play was completed at every different casino once.

I mention the method at this juncture because the number of different casinos in your round robin should be a function *of the number of casinos you choose as suitable for play*. If you find only a few such establishments, then the size of your round robin should be reduced to include *only* those casinos. *It's more important that you gamble in favorable casinos than play an extensive round robin schedule.*

If you are one of those players who can locate only a few favorable casinos...then stick with those at all costs, and use some of the other camouflage techniques described in Chapter 11 to protect yourself from harassment at the tables.

What About Cheating by the Casinos?

With all this talk of casinos manipulating their payoffs and hassling winners, you might be wondering just how far an establishment will go to ensure profits at their tables. Might a casino seek the ultimate house edge, and *cheat* you out of your bankroll? After all, with all that cutthroat competition after the gambling dollars, couldn't it be a temptation for some unscrupulous casino operators to fatten their profit margins by ordering a little hanky-panky at the tables?

Let me respond to the cheating issue in this way: every gambler must recognize that casino personnel— owners, managers, dealers—are human beings. And being human they are fallible. They can be tempted and they can be dishonest. In other words, they can cheat. And they have. In fact, the Gaming Control Board, which oversees gambling operations in Nevada, has closed several casinos for cheating over the years.

But... and this is a very important "but"—cheating in contemporary Las Vegas is extremely rare. So rare, in fact, that the average gambler will probably never encounter any in a lifetime of Vegas visits. Winning gamblers, particularly those who win *consistently* (e.g., blackjack counters), run a higher risk of being cheated, but they can avoid that risk by following the recommendations I will be making in a moment. In general, then, I am in agreement with Mario Puzo when he claims that "...present-day Vegas gambling is the most regulated and most honest that has ever existed."[31] In fact, when it comes to cheating in Vegas...there are many more incidents of players trying to cheat the house than vice versa!

Play In Vegas...and Play It Safe

Do not underestimate the psychological value of playing in an honest casino. When you don't have to worry about being cheated, you can play more effectively, concentrating on the game, rather than on the quick-fingered dealers. One major reason people gamble in Vegas in the first place is the peace of mind they have in knowing that things are on the "up and up." Give yourself a fair shake: never play in unregulated casinos where cheating is always a possibility. It just isn't a safe bet.

How to Defend Yourself Against Cheating

Your best defense is to limit your casino gambling *exclusively* to large, successful, legalized establishments in this country and abroad.* The odds on encountering cheating at these casinos are extremely small. The owners have too much to lose (revocation of a casino license can mean losses in the millions), and—considering the way most players gamble—there is no need to cheat because the games in themselves are a "license to steal."[32]

---

*Along these lines, gambling expert John Scarne recommends you ask yourself three questions before entering a casino: (1) *How long has the casino been operating?* The fact that a casino is crooked leaks out faster than you think, and only the honest ones stay in business year after year. (2) *Is the casino lavishly decorated or is it a makeshift affair?* The bigger the casino's investment in its quarters and furnishings, the more likely it is to be honest. Crooked games of dice, roulette and cards are usually found in small casinos, hotel rooms, private homes, at charity balls and conventions held behind closed doors. (3) *Is the casino well-patronized and doing good business, like the legal casinos in Nevada and Puerto Rico?* If so, you can almost be sure the operators aren't out to take you for every nickel they can get. A crowded casino is the best proof that it is honest. Don't be the only player, or one of the few players in a nearly-empty casino whose operators have worried looks on their faces! —Taken from *Scarne on Dice* by John Scarne, (Harrisburg, Pa. Stackpole Books, 1974), p. 133.

Another way to protect yourself against being cheated is to learn crooked moves and how to spot them. This is *extremely* difficult, what with the number of moves and the problems in detecting them. In fact, in the hands of a polished cheat, crooked moves are literally impossible to spot. John Scarne, the gambling authority and world-renowned magician, proves this quite conclusively when he tells people he's going to cheat at cards, does so right in front of them, yet they are unable to detect his moves. The hand is truly quicker than the eye. Particularly untrained eyes like mine . . . or yours.

Incidentally, if you want an "eye-opening" experience, read *Scarne's New Complete Guide to Gambling*. In this book, he provides a complete overview of cheating moves and how they're done. Once you finish reading the text you'll realize that if someone wants to cheat you, he'll be able to. Your best defense is to gamble in a place where dealers *won't* want to.

There is a third way to protect yourself against cheats, but you'll have to lose for a while before you can use it. Here's how the method works: each time you play, be alert for any *highly* unusual gambling results. If you find yourself losing *far more* than normal, or *greatly* in excess of what mathematical probabilities would predict, then you should quit at once and avoid playing in that establishment again.

Perhaps your losses weren't due to cheating—after all, mathematical probabilities do allow for highly unusual runs of cards and dice. Maybe you just ran into a mathematically rare event at the tables. There's really no way to tell (without actually *spotting* the crooked moves). But why take any chances? There's plenty of other places you can gamble . . . why stay at a casino where you consistently lose? If nothing else, maybe a change of playing locations will improve your psychological outlook, and get you back on the winning track.

Here's a final way to defend yourself against cheating: don't gamble too long in any one casino, particularly if you are a consistent winner. As I pointed out earlier, your chances of being cheated increase if you are a steady, big winner...particularly in blackjack where casino management *knows* the game can be beaten. By gambling an hour or less in each casino and then moving on, you make it difficult for casino management to assess your winning potential or to do anything about it. If you use the camouflage techniques presented in Chapter 11, your chances of being cheated due to your being a winner should be close to zero.

Using a Casino...On Your Terms

So far, so good. You've selected a casino and, because it's a reputable Vegas establishment, you're satisfied it's honest. Now what? Can you get into action, confident you've got the psychological advantage over the house? No...because you're only half-way there.

Psyching out Vegas involves more than choosing the casino(s) that offers you the best chance of winning. Even the most "player-favorable" gambling establishment will "do you in" if you don't know *how to use it properly*. This is because the dream merchants have carefully designed their casinos to put you at a psychological disadvantage, and reduce the effectiveness of your play. To turn things around and gain the mental edge, you will have to avoid the traps and pitfalls built into the casino "web" (see Chapter 3), and learn to use gambling establishments on your terms...or not at all.

The dream merchants have built their casinos to encourage *impulse gambling*—gambling which tends to lack control and organization. Thus, your first objective in properly using a casino is to avoid this kind of play at the tables.

Never walk into a gambling establishment on impulse.

That's hard to do in Vegas, where casinos surround you with 24-hour-a-day action. In England, where the player often gets a fairer shake at the tables, "...gaming clubs...are not allowed to advertise for members. Gaming by credit is forbidden. New members must wait 48 hours before gambling in any club they join. Cabaret acts, live music and dancing are not allowed in any gaming club. The purpose of these laws, as stated by the English, is to specifically protect people from gambling by whim."[33] Players in America, unfortunately, have no such protection...when it comes to controlling your gambling impulses, you're on your own.

One of the most dangerous times for impulse gambling occurs when you first arrive in Las Vegas. If you're like the typical tourist-gambler, you've been away from the tables for a long time...and now you want action—BAD! So, like a junkie relentlessly pursuing a fix, you dash off the airplane, hop a cab, rush into the casino and—even before you unpack your bags—hit the tables.

The casino owners love it! It's like turning an alcoholic loose in a distillery...except in this case, the player doesn't end up drunk...just broke. It makes me sad to think of all the players who lose their entire gambling stakes this way. Many are forced to return home without ever unpacking their bags. An entire vacation ruined... for what? For an uncontrolled impulse to gamble. It isn't worth it.

Don't let the hype, the neon, the jet lag, the need for action draw *you* into the casino before you're psychologically ready.

*Get acclimated to the Vegas environment
before you begin gambling.*

If possible, don't even gamble the first day you arrive in town (particularly if you arrive after 3:00 p.m.). But if you must have a go of it, at least check into your room and take a nice long shower or a dip in the pool first. Then visit the tables . . . refreshed and ready.

The next time you feel the need for impulse gambling the moment you arrive in Vegas . . . try this little assignment. When you're walking from your plane to the baggage claim area, take some time to observe the people preparing to *leave* Vegas. Look at their faces carefully. Note their expressions—the level of energy and optimism in their eyes. Think about the message all those faces are conveying. *That* should slow you down a bit!

When you eliminate impulse gambling from your life, you will achieve a major objective in your campaign to use casinos effectively. Another objective centers on the amount of time you spend in gambling establishments:

*Do not spend too much time gambling in a casino.
Three to four one-hour sessions per day are optimal.*

I know there is a temptation—particularly if you can't visit Vegas often—to gamble for long stretches at a time. Overcome this temptation. Gambling hour after hour makes you more vulnerable to casino "psychouts" and financial loss.

To play most effectively, you must be at your psychological and physical peak. There is no way this peak can be sustained in marathon sessions at the tables. Fatigue and stimulus bombardment combine to impair your senses . . . and your judgment. There is also a tendency to increase the size of your bets during long gambling sessions. Increased bets ward off the onset of boredom and keep excitement levels high. They also keep casino

177

profits high.

As in the case of impulse gambling, the casino owners aren't interested in helping you use their establishment effectively. They want you to stay around and gamble; the longer, the better. It gives them a better shot at your bankroll.

Did you ever wonder why casinos are windowless and without clocks? Well, now you know. The last thing the casino management wants you to be thinking about is the time of day (or night). As far as they're concerned, there's only one time in Las Vegas...and that's gambling time.

Want to fight the tendency to stay in casinos too long? The next time you visit Las Vegas, try these suggestions:

(1)   Make a gambling itinerary and stick to it (see Chapter 16). Know in advance when (how often, how long) you're going to be in the casinos. Setting aside specific times for gambling will help you combat the tendency to "lose track" of how long you've been playing.

(2)   Make plans to participate in as many non-gambling activities as you can. That way you won't have time on your hands, get bored, and hit the tables. (See Chapter 16 for a list of activities in and around Las Vegas.)

(3)   Wear a watch and be aware of time. Don't let a clockless city psych you into gambling too long.

Learning to control impulse gambling and extended playing time in the casinos will increase your chances for winning. So will the proper *psychological outlook*.

Never gamble in a casino
unless you have the proper mental attitude.

This is an objective that is essential to achieve if you

want to use casinos in an optimal way. How you can reach such an objective will be fully discussed in "Overcoming Your Psychological Governors," Chapter 13.

First, however, let me call your attention to one other tactic you'll want to employ if your aim is to use a casino rather than have a casino use you:

> *Always dispute any casino decision*
> *you do not agree with.*

Many players won't do this. They are too shy. Or too insecure. Or embarassed. Or just plain dumb. Whatever the reason, it doesn't justify their silence...or yours. Dealers aren't gods...they make mistakes like everyone else. But when mistakes are made in Vegas, they're made with *your* money. Therefore, don't be afraid to speak up if you have a question, challenge, or an objection. And do so *quickly*—before the situation changes through continued play.

Actually, it is financially irresponsible not to challenge any playing decision you disagree with. This is because most casinos have a "customer is right the first time" policy. What this means, in practice, is that the casino will automatically allow your claim the first time you dispute a payoff or some other dealer action. Don't expect such cooperative behavior the second time around, however!*

---

*There is an interesting story along these lines, involving the famous gambler, Nick the Greek. According to author Bill Friedman, the "Greek" had "...one outstanding characteristic as a gambler—he could perceive claim situations before the casino employees would. Since he only wagered on bets that had an average expected loss of less than two wagers an hour, he knew that he could obtain the advantage if could make two successful claims each hour. There were executives who never permitted his claims, many of which were obviously groundless. Their casinos lost his business, but other casinos occasionally let him make a successful claim. These executives realized that they still retained the advantage if they allowed him one claim an hour. The casino manager at one Strip hotel and another at a downtown Las Vegas casino timed Nick the Greek when he gambled, and they denied all claims until at least one hour had elapsed since they honored his last claim. This cut the casino's small advantage in half, but they attracted his high-limit business."[34]

Cleaning Out the Web

If you want to psych out Vegas, it is vital that you choose and use casinos properly. Gambling establishments are, after all, located in Las Vegas...and that gives the casino owners a home field advantage over you, the player from out of town. Your job is to cut that home field advantage to a minimum...or if possible, swing it in your favor.

Whenever you enter a casino remember that it has been designed to make you a loser. It is not a "safe house" where you can relax your vigilance...it is enemy territory where you must keep alert to keep financially alive.

In this chapter I have pointed out that some casinos are more dangerous than others to your economic well-being. *Your job is to choose and use those gambling establishments that afford you the best possible chances of winning at the tables.*

You might be in enemy territory—but at least you can

choose your own battlefield, and confront those casino forces where your chances for victory are greatest.

CHAPTER 13

OVERCOMING YOUR PSYCHOLOGICAL GOVERNORS

> "When my mind is ready to win . . . that's when I sit down to play."
> *—Professional Poker Player*

Regardless of where you decide to gamble or what type of game(s) you choose to play, you must have the proper mental attitude if you want to win. Without it, you'll be battling yourself as well as the odds . . . an altogether losing proposition. Achieving that all-important mental edge involves overcoming the *psychological governors* which restrict gambling effectiveness and reduce your chances of success in games of both chance and skill.

What Is a "Psychological Governor"?

Don't look for it in the dictionary. It is a term I created to refer to mental barriers which limit our gambling success to levels *less* than we are capable of achieving once these barriers are removed.

The concept of a "governor" is an interesting one. Those of you who are familiar with machines—particularly cars—will know that a governor is a small automatic device used to regulate speed. In automobiles, governors are normally employed to restrict driving speed to some predetermined upper limit and...this is important...that limit is always *less* than the rate of speed obtainable by the vehicle without the governor in use. In other words, a governor on an automobile serves to reduce *performance below potential*: the car can't, in effect, work to its full capacity.

A psychological governor does for a gambler what a mechanical governor does for an automobile: it restricts his range of performance and keeps his playing behavior below his playing potential.

There are three psychological governors we must identify, understand, and then disengage if we are to operate at peak gambling proficiency. Let us examine each one in turn.

PSYCHOLOGICAL GOVERNOR #1:
NEGATIVE THINKING

It's funny how insights seem to hit when you're least expecting them. Like after a tennis match. I was over at the public courts to work on my serve one day, when an old acquaintance named Jack sauntered up, said "Hello," and asked for a game. I agreed, hoping the competition would sharpen my play. As we rallied a bit to warm up, I noted with satisfaction that his strokes were smooth, his volleys crisp and sharp. Judging from his few minutes of practice, I guessed I'd be getting some great experience because Jack had all the earmarks of a formidable foe.

Maybe too formidable. Four games into the first set I was down 3-1, and my opponent was stepping to the service line. An ace and an easy put-away made the score 30-*love* and I had visions of a long afternoon. Then my seemingly invincible acquaintance made his first mistake—a double-fault. That made the score 30-15, hardly a moment of great crisis for Jack, yet I could tell he was disturbed.

He fidgeted around for several moments before his next serve, rubbing his hands over the rim of his racket and wiping the handle off against the side of his shorts. His next serve was a hummer, just wide. I signalled "out"... but Jack didn't seem to agree. He walked in a few steps, his face distorted in a scowl. "Are you sure?" he asked, a hint of disbelief in his voice.

"It was out," I replied flatly.

"Alright," he said, taking a deep breath. This time when he returned to the service line, he went through a whole series of gestures before he set himself for the serve.

"Long," I called.

This time the shot was clearly out, and Jack was clearly unhappy.

"Dammit to hell!" he cursed, causing a few heads to turn from the adjoining courts.

"You O.K.?" I asked, sensing his discomfort and trying to relax him.

"Yes, dammit...give me some balls," he responded belligerently, making tight little circles around the baseline.

Jack's next serve was in, but there was nothing on it. I

passed him and suddenly a 30-*love* game was add-out. I half expected an explosion from the other side of the net, but there was none. Instead Jack stood a few feet from the net, hands on hips, glaring at his racket. Then, without saying a word, he returned abruptly to back-court, and prepared for his next service.

The ball came at me like it had in the earlier games, a boomer serve that was beyond me almost before I got my racket on it. It was good luck that I even returned the shot, and it was incredible luck that the ball stayed in...nicking the backline and bounding to a stop against the screening behind the court.

What could I say? It was a one-in-a-thousand shot. "Shouldn't have had it," I muttered, almost guilty over my sudden turn in fortune. Jack just stood, shaking his head, looking at the spot where the ball had gone out.

"Service," I called, deciding that starting a new game might get things going and cool Jack down. Things got going but the only thing that got cooled down was Jack's game. What were once stinging forehands seemed like lobs; backhands that had kept me running seemed to follow me around like obedient children. It was the most incredible turnaround in a person's game I had ever seen.

I came back to win the first set 6-3, and was ahead 2-0 in the second when I decided to quit. Jack had turned on himself with a vengeance, and I just couldn't take any more of his self-abuse. As I began to walk off the court, Jack moved over to intercept me.

"Where are you going?" he asked. "The match isn't over yet."

"I know that," I replied, "but you don't need me. You play better against yourself than I ever could."

The Power of Negative Thinking

It was on my way home from the match that I had my insight. I had been thinking about Jack's collapse and how weak-willed he must have been to fall apart the way he did. That's when the realization hit.

Jack was not weak-willed—no weak will could bring a skilled body to ruin that effectively, that completely. Regardless of what I thought about the *correctness* of Jack's behavior, there was no doubt that he had a strong, well-developed will. . . *a will to lose.*

Unfortunately, this "will to lose" is not confined to competitive sports; there are thousands upon thousands of "Jacks" roaming the casinos of Las Vegas, falling apart and losing at the tables, just as convincingly as my acquaintance did on the tennis court.

Many years ago the well known clergyman and author, Norman Vincent Peale, wrote an optimistic book extolling the virtues of *positive thinking*. His message was basic and simple: if you believe, you can succeed. Peale was convinced that, if a person truly thought he could accomplish a given objective, then he would. . . and considering some of the "impossible" feats performed by true believers (i.e., making miraculous medical recoveries), Peale's convictions seemed reasonable. Such was the power of positive thinking.

Unfortunately, there is also the power of negative thinking. . . and it can wreak havoc with your chances of winning in Vegas. If one can believe and succeed, one can also *not* believe and fail, and therein lies the rub: negative thinking can create a "loser," a player who "chokes" under the least pressure, just as effectively as positive thinking can produce a "winner," the sort of individual who plays well when "the chips are down."

The negative-thinking gambler is a person with a psychological governor which can hamper his play at the tables. The more negative he is, the "lower" his psychological governor will be set. Put another way, the greater his negative thinking, the greater will be the gap between how well he is capable of playing and how well he actually plays.

Where Does Negative Thinking Come From?

Negative thinking is a psychological governor that comes into being when we unconsciously place limits on ourselves—limits that we come to believe exist because we had been told they exist by some respected source (e.g., parents, peers, teachers). Oftentimes these limiting beliefs are instilled in us at an early age. One of the most effective methods I know to encourage the development of a powerful, lifelong, negative thinker is telling a young child again and again: "You're no good . . . you'll never amount to anything." (Variations on the basic theme are allowed.) After a while, is it any wonder that a person *doesn't* amount to anything? He's been programmed to do poorly—to *think* he can't succeed—to *expect* he can't succeed . . . and his psychological governor is set for failure to make *sure* he won't succeed.

Sometimes cultural expectations can serve to develop negative thinking in a whole class of individuals who are affected by such expectations. Take women, for example. Although the (false) belief that women are less intelligent then men is fading, it is still true in many cases that females are taught from earliest childhood that they cannot beat males in head-to-head competition. Is it any wonder that a woman poker player, raised under such cultural directives, often "clutches" in card games with men, suddenly discovering that her game has "inexplicably" gone to pieces?

Remember, a person behaves in ways consistent with the image he has of himself, with the way he perceives himself to be. If a person thinks of himself as a loser, then he will gamble in a way that makes him a loser, and then when he becomes a loser, he will have proof he is a loser, which will make him lose even more. . . and so we have the familiar cycle of the self-fulfilling prophecy.

We Create Our Own Psychological Governors: We Can Also Eliminate Them

But the losing cycle can be broken. If we are negative thinkers, if our ability to perform is being kept in check by a psychological governor, *we can do something about it*. We weren't born with this governor; WE created it (even though we weren't aware of this). And if we created it, then we can also destroy it, freeing ourselves to operate at full power.

Our minds are wonderful instruments at our command, far more complex and adaptive than any computer known to science. The attitudes you hold about yourself, about your ability—they needn't stay fixed, etched "forever this way" into your psyche. They can be changed. . . and will be, with some effort on your part. And this is true even for those people with very negative thinking patterns. Ironically, it is these people—like Jack the tennis player—who have the greatest potential to change for the better. Think about it: if a man like Jack possesses a mind powerful enough to create such a potent psychological governor, then his mind is also powerful enough to wipe it away, to replace extremely negative thoughts with equally powerful, positive ones.

189

How Do You Know If You Are a Negative Thinker?

This is not always an easy thing to determine, particularly since these governors represent limits we *unconsciously* place on ourselves—often early in our
childhoods, when memories are sketchy and vague at
best. At present there is no easy-to-take, valid test that
can accurately tell us whether we are positive or
negative thinkers. However, there are certain kinds of
behaviors and outlooks that seem to be associated with
negative thinkers. Read the following statements and
think about them. Do they describe you? If you answer
"yes," the possibility that you have negative thinking
tendencies is increased.

First, in the realm of gambling:

* When you sit down to play, you don't really expect
  to win (or you set your goal at "breaking even").
* If you start losing, you think you won't be able to
  come back.
* If you start winning, you suspect you'll lose it all
  back.
* In games of skill (i.e., poker), you tend to lose
  against players who seem to be no more talented
  than you.
* Your gambling has a tendency to fall apart if you
  make a few bad bets.
* You tend to become *self*-abusive during play, particularly if things don't go your way.
* In games of skill with a *new* opponent you know
  nothing about, you tend to assume you won't do
  that well.
* In games of skill, if you lose slightly to someone
  you're playing with for the first time, you figure you

won't be able to beat that person the next time you confront him/her across the table.

* On an important roll of dice, or a pivotal hand of cards, you figure you're going to lose.

Now, here are some general statements about your psychological outlook. How closely do they describe you?

* You tend to have self-doubt rather than self-confidence.
* You don't normally like to set yourself difficult obstacles to overcome.
* You feel that other people doubt your ability to perform adequately.
* When it comes to your outlook on life, you are generally more pessimistic than optimistic.
* In your life you've probably met people whom you consider to be "confident"—people who have "faith in themselves." You feel that you are not like them.
* Your assessment of yourself tends to be generally more negative than positive (e.g., you tend to tear yourself down more than you build yourself up).

Overcoming Negative Attitudes In the Casino

Getting a person who sees himself as a loser to enter a casino with a positive, winning attitude is no easy task. If his negative feelings are too pervasive and deeply rooted, it will take a total personality "overhaul" in order to change him, which, of course, is well beyond the scope of this book.

Fortunately, very few gamblers are so negative about themselves that they cannot achieve a positive attitude at the tables. To gain that all-important psychological edge that goes hand-in-hand with the proper winning attitude, take the steps I have recommended:

(1) *Understand those casino tactics designed to psych you into losing.* (Chapters 1-6.) Forewarned is forearmed.

(2) *Play "tough."* Know the game you are playing, and play it smart. Play only those games and wagers where you have a gambling chance of winning (see Chapter 8). Ideally, concentrate on blackjack, where the odds are in *your* favor. Nothing builds a positive attitude like winning... and nothing helps winning like a game with the percentages on *your* side.

(3) *Develop self-control at the tables.* The material in Chapters 9 and 12 will help you do this. Knowing you can maintain self-discipline in the face of casino pressures will greatly enhance your self-confidence and potential for winning.

(4) *Learn to overcome the three psychological governors discussed in this chapter.*

(5) *Do NOT play if you want to lose (Chapter 6), or if you are a degenerate gambler (Chapter 18).* Playing under these conditions will only fuel your losing ways and heighten your negative attitudes about gambling and yourself.

PSYCHOLOGICAL GOVERNOR #2: VEGAS "BURNOUT"

Las Vegas is a giant pep pill, a kind of electrical jolt designed to course through your body and keep you charged up for three and four days of nonstop revelry and gambling. There are no clocks on the walls to tell you it's late, no windows in the casinos to remind you the sun has set. If you're lucky, you'll experience Las Vegas "burnout" once you return home, moping around for a week like a person coming down from amphetamines. If you're *not* lucky, you'll begin experiencing burnout while you're still *in* Vegas. The problem is that you probably won't notice the symptoms: the reduced concentration; the poorer judgment; the sloppier, more aggressive betting. You'll be too psyched up by the Vegas energy to notice. It's kind of like the football player who cracks a rib during play, but is so high on the game he doesn't feel pain until the final gun sounds.

One thing you will notice, however: the price you've paid for your folly. Gambling is a very exhausting activity, particularly if you're trying to count cards at the blackjack table or keep track of several *come* bets at craps. Action is the name of the game in Vegas, and it comes fast and furious. If you don't learn to pace yourself in this animated environment, your playing skils and your bankroll will suffer. The casino managers realize this, and do what they can to keep you hyped up and gambling at a frenetic pace. *Don't fall prey to their "psychout."* Don't you be like the diver who, bedazzled by the beauty of the deep, suddenly realizes he has run out of air.

How To Turn Out Burnout

If you want to gamble at full proficiency, you must follow certain rules to guard against Vegas burnout. Observing there rules will require a little planning and scheduling before you come to Vegas, and a lot of self-control once you arrive. Here are the rules:

(1) Set up a gambling schedule before you leave on your trip, and stick to it once you arrive in Las Vegas.

(2) Do not gamble more than three or four times a day.

(3) Do not gamble more than an hour at a time.

(4) Try not to gamble immediately after you arrive in town—give your body and mind a chance to adjust to the new environment. Also, be wary of "jet lag" if you've just completed a long flight to Las Vegas.

(5) Try and get a reasonable amount of sleep in Las Vegas.

(6) Do not gamble immediately after a heavy meal.

(7) Do not gamble while under the influence of drugs or alcohol.

(8) Do not play when you feel "stale," tired, listless or rundown.

(9) Stop gambling immediately if you feel hassled or emotionally distraught for any reason.

(10) Do not play when you feel sick (even *slightly* sick).

(11) Do not gamble with people who affect your play in a negative manner.

(12) Do not play when you find it difficult to concentrate.

(13) Do not play so long that your senses become dulled.

(14) Look in a mirror before each gaming session. If you appear "wired or tired," steer clear of the tables.

(15) Restrict your gambling to casinos that best fulfill your psychological needs (see Chapter 12).

(16) Gamble at times when you are psychologically *and* physically at your peak (see below).

Discovering YOUR Best Time To Gamble

In the past twenty-five years, scientists have become increasingly impressed with the range and diversity in patterns of human behavior that seem to follow regular "cycles" or "rhythms," called "biorhythms." An example of such a "biorhythm" is the menstrual cycle.

The fact that the human body follows regular cycles enables us to predict what our physical and mental states will be at given times. If, for example, you note at what periods of the day you feel energetic and at what times you feel drowsy, a pattern will eventually emerge, indicating your daily *alertness* cycle. Once you identify your own biorhythms and their patterns, you can use this information to function more effectively on a day-to-day-basis.

As an example, consider this question: "When is my best time to gamble?" According to Rule #12 above, you should gamble at times when you are psychologically at your peak. But when is that? Knowing your biorhythms can help answer this question.

To illustrate, let us assume that when you were reflecting about your body cycles, you discovered that between 8:00 a.m. and noon you are generally:

* drowsy
* lethargic
* dull
* easily distracted

Let us assume further that between 8:00 p.m. and midnight you are generally:

* awake
* active
* alert
* able to concentrate

When do you think it would be best for you to sit down and play blackjack, or get into a fast-action crap game?

Pinpointing Your Biorhythms

When a person wants to find out what his body rhythms are he uses a method known as *body charting*. This is simply a "log" or "diary" for recording and keeping track of your hourly, daily, monthly, and even yearly body rhythms. Now it is sometimes true that fluctuations in some body rhythms are so readily apparent to us that we needn't chart them to know when they're most likely to occur. "I'm an early riser—been so all my life," might be the observation of a person who knows his body cycles when it comes to sleep/waking patterns. If this is true in your case, then simply being aware of the patterns and their fluctuations will be sufficient to take advantage of them.

Yet, in many cases we are *unaware* of our body cycles, and under these conditions body charting is the best way to uncover them...and the information they provide. Fluctuations in our moods, for instance, are often difficult to spot without the aid of body charting. So are changes in our physical responses (e.g., energy level, reaction time), when the cycles for these bodily states are irregular or of long duration.

Fortunately, body charting does not require elaborate machinery. A person simply decides what mood or physical state he wishes to chart, then keeps track of its occurrence on a piece of paper, in a makeshift diary, or on any other recording device. The technique is simple, practical, and available to anyone with a pencil, paper, and a little patience.

Your Gambler's Body Rhythm Diary

There are many ways to chart your body cycles, as well

as many different cycles you could choose to chart—what I want to do is make your task as inexpensive, convenient and simple as possible, while concentrating on those biorhythms that will help you determine your best time to gamble. A sample diary page is presented below.

Sample Page From a
Gambler's Body Rhythm Diary

DATE_____TIME_____CHART #_____

****

ENERGY

Lethargic --*Active*

| Much more Lethargic than normal | Energy level About normal | Much more Active than normal |

****

CONCENTRATION

Easily
*Distracted*_____*Focus Attention*
Able To

| Much more easily distracted than normal | Concentration about normal | Much more able to focus attention than normal |

****

TENSION LEVEL

Relaxed ---*Tense*

| Much more relaxed than normal | Tension level about normal | Much tenser than normal |

****

INTELLECTIVE FUNCTION

Sluggish ————————————————————————————*Sharp*

Much more	Intellective	Much Sharper
sluggish	function	than normal
than normal	about normal	

****

SELF-CONFIDENCE

Confident————————————————————————————*Insecure*

Much more	Self-confidence	Much more
confident	about normal	insecure
than normal		than normal

****

WAKEFULNESS

Fatigued ————————————————————————————*Awake*

Much more	Wakefulness	Much more
fatigued	About normal	awake than
than normal		normal

****

MOOD

Good Mood————————————————————————————*Bad Mood*

Much more	Mood about	Much more
in good mood	normal	in bad mood
than normal		than normal

Feel free to alter the page to your individual needs as you see fit. Now, here are some instructions for using your body rhythm diary:

One hour after you awaken, and every three hours thereafter until bedtime, evaluate your moods and physical states as listed in FIGURE 3. Use a new sheet for each evaluation. If you feel that filling out the "log" every three hours is too much of a hassle, then wait longer intervals before filling it out (say every four, five or six hours). There is no magic number of times you should make entries in your diary; what is important is that you generate sufficient data points for accurately mapping the biorhythms(s) in question.

Some people have trouble filling out their body rhythm diary because they're unclear about the definitions of the various moods and physical states listed in FIGURE 3. This is not surprising, as these terms have many different meanings to different individuals. For our purposes, utilize the definitions below when filling out your Body Rhythm Diary.

(1) ENERGY: Refers to the amount of *physical* zest or "pep" you have. When you feel "run down," or physically "drained," your energy level would be low *(Lethargic)*. When you feel "charged" and "full of gusto," your energy level would be high *(Active)*.

(2) CONCENTRATION: Refers to the ability to zero in on an activity and keep it in the center of your attention. When you are unable to focus your attention successfully, your concentration level would be low *(Easily Distracted)*. When you are able to rivet your attention, your concentration level would be high *(Able To Focus Attention)*.

* If you would like a pre-printed set of 90 Daily Charts with tables for tabulation send $4.95 plus $1.00 postage and handling to: Gambler's Body Rhythm Diary, Gambling Times, 1018 N. Cole Avenue, Hollywood, CA 90038.

(3) TENSION LEVEL: Refers to the amount of nervousness you feel. When you feel "loose," calm and mentally at ease, your tension level would be low *(Relaxed)*. When you feel uneasy, under stress and jittery, your tension level would be high *(Tense)*.

(4) INTELLECTIVE FUNCTION: Refers to how well you can "use your mind" at a given point in time. When you can't seem to think clearly, quickly and/or creatively, your intellective function would be low *(Sluggish)*. When your mind is in "high gear," and your thinking has clarity and power, your intellective function would be high *(Sharp)*.

(5) SELF-CONFIDENCE: Refers to how much you "believe in yourself"...how much self-assurance you have. When you have faith in your decisions, and believe you can "lick the world," your self-confidence would be high *(Confident)*. When you doubt your ability to succeed and question your worth, your self-confidence would be low *(Insecure)*.

(6) WAKEFULNESS: Refers to the degree of alertness you are experiencing at a given time. When you feel drowsy (tired), your wakefulness level would be low *(Fatigued)*. When you are vigilant and feel wide-awake, your wakefulness level would be high *(Awake)*.

(7) MOOD: Refers to your general disposition—how you are feeling—at a given time. If you are happy and in good spirits, your mood would be positive *(Good Mood)*. If you feel sad and "down in the dumps," your mood would be negative *(Bad Mood)*.

Here's an example of how to make an entry in your Body Rhythm Diary. Let's use the ENERGY question for illustrative purposes. If (say at 2:00 p.m.) you feel much more lethargic than is customary for you during a normal waking day, then you would put an "X" on the left side of the continuum above the response, "Much less energy than normal." Remember, also, that when you say, "I feel much less energy than normal"...that "normal" refers to the *average* level of energy you usually experience from day to day. In other words, if at 2:00 p.m. you "feel much less energy than normal," you don't mean compared to other days at 2:00 p.m., but rather to what your normal wakefulness level is over the entire day.

By duplicating FIGURE 3 for the number of days you plan to plot your body cycles, you can construct your personalized diary (number the pages consecutively, and use new ones each time you make an entry).

You will get the most out of your body rhythm diary if you use it correctly. Here are two important points you should keep in mind as you begin your body charting:

(1) *Length of the diary:* "How many days should I chart my body cycles?" This is a question I'm frequently asked. Some cycles are more difficult to track than others. A rule-of-thumb recommendation is this: A good sampling should embrace a period of ninety days, or three months. The minimum acceptable time limit is thirty days, or one month.

(2) *The backwards glance:* Once you have completed a chart, do not look at it again until you have completed all of the charts and are ready to tally your results. If you do look back, you may unconsciously alter your answers to fit ideas of what you think your rhythms "should be."

When you have charted your body rhythms for a suitable period of time, go back over the data points and see if any patterns emerge. If you find that some of your moods and/or physical states do occur with predictable regularity, then you will be in a position to use that information in determining your best time(s) to gamble. If, for example, you find that a majority of your physical states tend to "peak out" at regular intervals during the day, you could then schedule casino visits to take place at these times. You could also discover, upon examining your body charts, that your physical states "peak out" for two or three days at a time...and then they might recede for days or weeks...only to return to the peak level at predictable intervals. Again, you could take advantage of this harder-to-recognize physical pattern so that you could bunch your gambling activities into your two-to-three-day "up" periods.

Some individuals use their body rhythm logs in quite a different fashion. They fill out a chart each time before they gamble, then compare their gaming results with the data on their charts. What they are looking for is any pattern of responses in their diaries which corresponds to their patterns of winning or losing at the tables. For instance, assume (highly unlikely) that, after numerous chart entries and gambling sessions, a player was able to determine that his best winning sessions usually occurred when he was close to "normal" on his various moods and physical states. This might suggest (although correlation is not causation) that his best bet would be to gamble when his moods and physical states were not extreme in either the positive or negative direction. Another player might discover (also highly unlikely) that his best winning sessions occurred when he was high in energy level *and* tension, and that he didn't do so well when his energy was high and his tension level was low. The conclusion: it might be best if he steered clear of the table unless he was both active and tense at the same time.

If you want to use your body rhythm charts in this manner, do so with a healthy skepticism concerning the results. Remember that correlation is not causation—and that any relationships you find should be thoroughly tested at the tables to make sure they are valid and not due to chance factors or self-fulfilling prophecies.

When you first begin body charting it might seem like a chore. In practice, however, it can become an intriguing adveenture. Most of us are so out of touch with ourselves that any extensive attempt at self-observation produces many unexpected experiences and insights. Most important, if you undertake a diligent program of body charting, you will gain an additional tool for psyching out Vegas and improving your chances for winning at the tables.

PSYCHOLOGICAL GOVERNOR #3: SUPERSTITIOUS BEHAVIOR THAT RESULTS IN DYSFUNCTION

Imagine the following situation. A game of key importance is in progress. The players are battling for the crucial victory. Suddenly time is called. One team demands that the ball in play be replaced. An hour passes before a new ball can be found and put into the game. I ask you: what could have been so wrong with the ball that a team could call for its replacement and hold up the contest for an hour in the process. Might it have been an imperfection in the shape of the ball? A rip in the cover? Incorrect air pressure inside? No. It was none of those things. The ball was replaced because, according to the protesting team, it was *bewitched.*

That's right . . . *bewitched.* It turns out that in Tanzania, where this game was played, hexes are an important part of the sports scene. So important, in fact, that according to Job Omino, secretary of the Kenya Football Association, 95% of the 200 teams in Kenya have witch doctors in their employ. One team alone spent $3,062.40

(a lot of money in Kenyan currency) witch-doctoring games during a season. And how do the witch doctors ply their trade? They use "...all sorts of stuff. Often herbal mixtures, tree sap and a touch of pig fat are smeared on the players and spells are put on the game ball."[35] Prayers are also used, as are occasional sacrifices of live goats and chickens.

Sounds silly...doesn't it? Grown men refusing to play with a ball because they think it's "bewitched." Other grown men paying thousands to make sure it is "bewitched" in the first place. Well, it might sound silly, but before you pass any final judgment on just how silly you find such behavior to be, why not take a moment to consider the actions of Bill, a red-blooded American gambler.

Bill is a high-rolling, fast-betting player. I met him one night at a Strip casino and we exchanged small talk while shooting craps. Bill liked action. He'd bet the pass line and then place all the numbers—hoping the dice would stay out awhile before the inexorable 7 showed. It was poor percentage gambling, and Bill was paying the full price. For a half-hour his bankroll got torn apart; 7's seemed to be showing every four or five rolls. He just grimaced, signed more markers, and tried to weather the storm. "I'm waiting for the big hand," he explained, and put some more black chips on the layout.

Well, the big hand *did* show. A well dressed young man across the table began throwing number after number—the kind of hand designed to get Bill back on track...fast.

"The seven's gone to sleep," Bill chortled gleefully, and pressed his bets up.

The young man proceeded to make four straight

passes, and that made Bill a true believer. Tossing in a handful of chips, he went for the chandeliers. "Sixty-four hundred across," he instructed the dealer, who put ten black chips on the 4, 5, 9, and 10, and twelve chips on the 6 and 8.

"Now let's have some numbers...*num*bers," Bill shouted, "you can do it, shooter."

"Eight...the point is eight," intoned the stickman as the young man came out on his fifth pass. Everyone was pushing bets out on the table, trying to ride the lucky hand to the hilt. A few more passes and everyone would be healthy, including Bill.

Then it happened. The young man tossed the dice with too much power, and one cube bounded off the table onto the casino floor.

"Dice down...no roll," called the stickman.

Bill exhaled sharply. "Damn!" he exclaimed angrily, and turning to the dealer he said, "take me down."

The dealer returned Bill's sixty-four hundred dollars worth of chips.

"What's the matter?" I asked.

"A dice on the floor means a seven's at the door," he replied somberly, and watched as the shooter threw again...the point 10.

I glanced at Bill. He remained motionless.

The shooter threw two more numbers. If Bill had "stayed up" he would have made over $4,000. Bill looked miserable but he refused to bet. "I know a seven's coming," he muttered to no one in particular, "the dice went off the table."

Bill was right. A 7 did come up. The only problem, from his point of view, was that it took twelve more rolls to do so—nine of which were point numbers. Remaining out of action had cost Bill over $10,000!

* * *

Now I ask you: is there really a difference between the good, old American gambling superstition that a 7 follows when dice are tossed off the table and the "silly" Kenyan hex? Is a Tanzanian player who calls for a new ball because the old one is hexed any more or less "silly" than the American gambler who calls off his working bets because a die hit the floor?

The simple truth of the matter is that all over the world athletes and gamblers are superstitious—they believe that their play can be influenced by factors that have absolutely nothing to do with their own competence or that of their opponents.

Normally, such beliefs are relatively innocuous human diversions. After all, what harm can come from a gambler wearing his "lucky shirt" to the tables, or refusing to roll the dice unless he clicks them together three times first? No harm—unless those beliefs affect his play in a deleterious manner, in a way that decreases his chances for winning and financial gain.

I have seen competent blackjack and poker players "come apart" because they think they are "jinxed." I have seen baccarat and dice players go from sensible to ruinous betting behavior because of a "sign." In these cases, superstitions and superstitious behaviors can be *very harmful;* in fact, they can sometimes bring about the downfall of otherwise "tough" players.

There is no room in a casino for superstitious behavior that makes a player dysfunctional—it is a psychological governor that can hold you back from peak performance.* If you must cart a rabbit's foot around to the tables, go ahead. But don't go to pieces if you misplace the hairy appendage, and don't start making "hare" brained bets because your lucky charm tells you

206

to. Winners don't bet that way . . . and I want you to be a winner.

*Be particularly wary of superstitious behavior if you are involved in games of skill. In poker, for instance, superstitious behavior can telegraph your hand and your strategy to opponents; further, your opponents can use your supersititious beliefs to psych you out and weaken your play (see Chapter 14).

CHAPTER 14

CASINO POKER:
ACES AND EIGHTS FOR THE UNWARY

> "If you understand how a
> man plays poker, you'll under-
> stand the man."
> —*Old Poker Adage*

Ten years ago this chapter wouldn't have done you much good: casino poker games in Vegas were as scarce as a flush in five card stud. Now five card stud is scarce, but casino poker rooms are as plentiful as a kibbitzer's recommendations.

Some Las Vegas Poker Statistics [36]

You needn't worry about finding an open seat when you arrive for some poker action in the gambling city! There are—as of 1980—more than thirty-five casino

cardrooms in operation along the Las Vegas Strip and in
Casino Center downtown. Some of these cardrooms are
small one- or two-table operations; others are literally
poker palaces, with up to twenty tables in action. The
average size cardroom contains from four to seven tables
and, in all, there are just under 250 poker tables to handle the traffic of locals and visitors alike.

What about the games? There are many kinds of poker
games, some more popular than others. Further, poker
games fluctuate in their popularity—for example, draw
poker used to be very popular; now you're lucky if you
can find a game. In Vegas, the poker games that are
played mirror the current tastes of the poker-playing
public. Popular games are highlighted; less popular
games are a rarity. Currently (1980), two poker games
"rule the roost": seven card stud and hold 'em. The overwhelming popularity of these games can be seen by
checking out Table 14-1. The implications are clear:
seven card stud and hold'em aren't "the only games in
town"... but you're going to have to do some looking if
your poker pleasure happens to run along different lines.

TABLE 14-1
DOWNTOWN LAS VEGAS POKER ROOMS

CASINO	TABLE	GAMES	LIMITS
El Cortez	4	S.S.,H.E.	1&2
Fremont	16	L.B.,S.S.,H.E.	1&2, 2&4, 3&6
Four Queens	9	S.S.,H.E.	1&2, 1&4, 5&10
Golden Nugget	12	S.S.,H.E.	1&2, 2&4, 3&6, 5&10, 15&30, 20&40
Horseshoe	side games offered only during World Series tournament		
Holiday Int'l	6	S.S.,H.E.	1&3, 2&4
Las Vegas Club	4	S.S.	1&3
Lady Luck	4	S.S.,H.E.	1&3, 2&4
Mint	10	L.B., S.S., H.E.	1&3, 2&4
Union Plaza	7	S.S,H.E.	1&3, 3&6, 5&10
Western Hotel	2	S.S.	1&2, 1&3

BOULDER HIGHWAY POKER ROOMS

Nevada Palace	2	S.S.	1&3
Sam's Town	4	S.S.	1&3, 2&4

LAS VEGAS STRIP POKER ROOMS

Ambassador	1	S.S.	1&3
Aladdin	9	S.S.,H.E.	1&3, 2&4, 3&6, 5&10
Bingo Palace	6	S.S.,H.E.	2&4, 3&6
Barbary Coast	6	S.S.	1&3, 2&4
Castaways	2	dealer's choice	limits vary
Caesars Palace	11	S.S.	1&3, 2&4, 1&5, 5&10
Continental	8	S.S., H.E.	1&3, 2&4
Desert Inn	7	S.S.	1&3
Dunes	10	H.L.S.,RZ.,S.S.,H.E.	all limits up to 300 & 600 no limit hold 'em
Holiday Inn	8	S.S.	1&2, 1&3
Hacienda	4	S.S.	1&2, 2&4, 3&6
Imperial Palace	6	S.S.	1&3, 2&4
Landmark	5	S.S.,H.E.	1&3, 2&4, 3&6
Maxim	4	S.S.	1&3
Marina	4	S.S.	limits vary
MGM Grand	16	S.S.	1&3, 2&4, 3&6, 5&10
Shenandoah	6	H.L.S.,RZ.,S.S.	1&4, 5&10
Silver City	7	S.S.,H.E.	1&2, 1&5, no limit hold 'em
Silver Slipper	6	S.S.,H.E.	limits vary
Silver Nugget	2	S.S.	1&3
Stardust	20	L.B.,RZ.,H.E.	all limits up to 50 & 100 pot limit hold 'em
Treasury	4	S.S.,H.E.	1&3, 2&4, no limit hold 'em pot limit hold 'em
Tropicana	7	S.S.,H.E.	limits vary
Vegas World	4	S.S.	1&3

L.B. is lowball; H.E. is hold em; and S.S. is seven card stud poker

H.L.S. is hi to split, RZ is razz poker.

© 1980 Gambling Times
Reprinted by permission
of the publisher

Do you have to be rich to sit in a Vegas poker game? Definitely not. Of course, there are high limit games to fit any taste and billfold (go to the Dunes casino and see for yourself!), yet an examination of the posted betting limits indicates that the majority of games are in the $1-$5 range for seven card stud and the $2-$6 bracket for hold 'em.

Should You Play Poker In a Las Vegas Cardroom?

It's probably every Saturday-night-poker buff's dream to come to Vegas and clean up big in the cardrooms. Kind of like a farm club ballplayer wanting to prove his mettle in the majors. Some of these would-be giant-killers even see themselves moving to Vegas and living off their poker winnings...a little golf or racquetball, a massage at the health club, a dinner show at the Dunes, a few hours of cards, a woman or two...*the good life*.

Well, before you reserve a moving van, permit me a few observations. Yes, it *is* possible to win at poker in Las Vegas...if you're good, *extremely good*. But it is very difficult to win with any regularity (let alone make a living from poker) due to two factors: the competition at the tables and the casino charges for playing (the "rake").

The Competition

I'm a decent tennis player but I don't expect to go up against Bjorn Borg and win. In Las Vegas, the finest poker players in the world ply their trade. For them, poker is more than a once-a-week ritual...it's their way of life. So tell me, when you sit down across from them at the tables, why do you think you should come away with the money?

Please don't misunderstand. I want you to win in Vegas . . . at whatever game(s) you play. But when it comes to winning at poker, it's crucial you understand the caliber of competition you'll be facing. Poker is a game of skill, and skill will separate the winners from the losers quickly enough. Unless you can match or exceed the talents of Vegas poker regulars, don't expect to sit down at the card tables and win *over the long haul* (anyone can get lucky for a few sessions, but luck doesn't last forever).

"Well," you might be saying, "all the people who play poker in Vegas can't be pros—what about the visitors like myself?" It is true that tourists and visiting gamblers do make up a sizeable proportion of the poker-playing participants in Vegas, but remember, it only takes *one* pro at a poker table to clean up all around. Remember, also, that the competition gets rougher as the stakes go higher. You might not find many (if any) pros at the $1.00-$3.00 tables, but hit the higher limit games and you'll think you just entered the World Series of Poker.

The Rake

Did you ever wonder *why* poker has become such a frequently-played casino game? It's not a public service to the card-playing public! Your friendly cardroom is there because it can turn a handsome profit for the casino—to the tune of a million dollars a year, and more. Now that's *serious* money . . . and what makes it even

213

more serious is it's *your* money. "It's the price you pay for the right to play," is the way one poetic cardroom manager put it. The casino supplies the cardroom, the equipment and a dealer; and for that service you pay a "seat tariff". . . a kind of "rental" fee for using their facilities. The casino owners don't care if you win or lose; they aren't gambling against you. All they want you to do is sit down and play—because *that* is when they make their profit.

There are two ways this casino "charge" is levied. One way is a *flat-rate* charge, for which you pay a specific, set amount for every hour (or half-hour) you play. This type of charge is not very common in Vegas and when it is found at all, it is usually in big money games. The majority of casinos get their "vig" a second way, by taking a percentage of the action at the tables. This method is known as *"the rake"*. . . an appropriate term, as the dealer "rakes" in a certain percentage of money from each pot. Cardroom personnel will tell you, if you ask, what the amount of the rake is. It is important that you know this information, as the rake can vary significantly from cardroom to cardroom and game to game (depending on the betting limits).

Let me tell you: I have sat in on many poker games and observed the dealer "rake" in the house cut. It was done so subtly—with such finesse—that it was hardly noticeable. . . even when I was looking for it. But believe me, it does take place. . . and while the dealer is raking in the green, you're getting raked over the coals!

In many ways, the casino rake is similar to the track takeout on winning bets. Every time you collect any money (e.g., cash a ticket or win a pot), you are paid off in the amount that's left AFTER the track or casino have taken their cut off the top. What this means to you—the prospective poker player—is that, if you want to win, you must first beat the skilled players sitting around you and then you must beat the house rake that's levied against you. This is a very formidable one-two punch— and in the long run it will knock out all but the most talented players.

Which brings us full circle to our original question: "Should you play poker in a Las Vegas cardroom?" If, after considering the kind of competition and house "take-out" you will face, you still want a shot at the tables—then I say, "go ahead." But do so cautiously. Start at the lower limit tables, then work your way up. If you can't win against dollar bettors, there's no reason to expect you'll do better in higher stakes games where the competition is keener.

Some Recommendations For Winning In Casino Poker Rooms

The next time you visit a Vegas cardroom, or any other legalized poker establishment, keep the following recommendations in mind. They won't guarantee a good run of cards, but they will increase your winning potential at the tables.

(1) Know the game you're playing, and know it *well.* Poker is a game of skill. In a competitive setting it is like any other skill: the better you are at it, the better you'll do at it.

(2) Do not begin playing poker until you specifically understand the "local" rules in force. Poker rules and betting procedures vary from locale to locale, so be sure to check *all* playing regulations before you "ante up."

(3) Casino cardrooms, like casinos in general, vary in

atmosphere and playing conditions (see Chapter 12). It is important that you familiarize yourself with as many of them as you can before you start playing...that way, you'll be able to select the one(s) most favorable for your particular gambling needs and playing preferences.

(4) Frequent those establishments that have the lowest "rake" for the kind of game(s) and betting limit(s) you play.

(5) Try not to play against the same opponents for any length of time. Las Vegas poker regulars make big profits from spotting player "tells" (non-verbal tip-offs to what a person is holding), and they use this information to win hands. Most amateur players "telegraph" their hands without realizing it. They might get away with such behavior in their local weekly game, but in Vegas they'll be drawn and quartered. Also, Vegas poker regulars are quick to spot a player's betting patterns. The longer you play with these resident cardsharps, the better they're able to "size you up." Don't let them get a line on your play...keep on the move.

(6) Although the likelihood of a Vegas poker dealer cheating you is *extremely* remote, the same can't be said for your fellow players. It is not the dealer's responsibility to protect you. Be wary and keep your eyes open—poker is an adversarial game, and the enemy is all around you. Keep your hole cards protected at all times. Show them to *no one*—even the player next to you who has thrown in his cards. He might have a "live" partner who is still in action, and then signal him what you hold. Or he might use the information to get a line on how you play. Also, watch out for the "railbirds"...non-players who stand outside the cordoned-off poker

area. Sometimes these "spectators" are paid by players in *your* game to check out (and transmit) what you're holding. And be careful about leaving chips scattered about in easy reach of other players. If you're going to sustain a loss, at least make sure it happens in the pot. . . not along the sidelines!

(7) As indicated earlier, test out your poker-playing skills in low limit games at first. If you win, then move up gradually into higher stakes games. Don't ever play "over your head": it's more fun to win at $3.00-$6.00 than lose at $5.00-$10.00. Your goal should be to play at the highest betting level you can afford where you can consistently be a winner.

(8) During poker sessions, follow all the relevant principles of play already presented in this book. Be particularly careful about how long you play. Many visiting gamblers aren't used to non-stop poker games. They hit Vegas and "go crazy," playing hour after hour until they are emotionally and mentally drained. More than likely their funds will be drained too. Keep a tight rein on your poker-playing time—it will help you obtain the winning edge.

* * *

The game of poker is wonderfully subtle and complex. It is a game of mathematical odds and psychological calculations, an opportunity to learn more about yourself, and human nature in general. It is also a game of profit and loss, and it's a treacherous money trap for the unprepared. To be a successful poker player you must play the game with the respect it deserves. If you're willing to play that way, then you'll have a gambling chance of winning.

CHAPTER 15

ROBERTS' RULES FOR WINNING

> "What general ventures forth
> in battle without a strategy
> well in mind?"
> —*Anonymous*

For me, there are few things as exciting as the anticipation of Las Vegas, those last few hours before you arrive in the Gambling City. It is a time for optimism and challenge—the feeling of an impending battle to be won.

During this tumultuous time it is difficult to think about your playing strategy...to review your overall game plan. Yet, it is vitally important that you do so.

Never venture into Vegas without first
reviewing your overall gambling strategy.

I normally do this during my flight to Vegas. Such a review doesn't take long—around half an hour—just enough time to refresh my memory and lock my playing strategy firmly in mind.

This chapter is designed to help you undertake such a review. It provides a rule by rule summary of the things you should be doing to improve your play and to gain the psychological edge when you gamble. This chapter is purposely brief so you can review the major concepts of effective play in a few minutes...without having to reread the entire book. Hopefully, this will encourage you to study the chapter each time you visit Las Vegas.

To facilitate your review, I have subdivided the rules into sections which approximate various chapters in the book. That way, if you want more information on a certain rule, you'll have a better idea of where to look in the text.

Your Rules For Psyching Out Vegas

PLAYING IT SMART (Chapter 8)

RULE 1:   Develop a playing strategy *before* you come to Las Vegas. Once you sit down at the tables you should have a plan of action ready to follow.

RULE 2:   Practice gambling at home before you wager in a casino. Make sure you can win at the kitchen table before you try your hand at the casino table.

RULE 3:   Have a complete understanding of the game(s) you play, or don't play at all.

RULE 4:   Rely on skill...not on luck.

RULE 5:   When playing games of chance, your best bets in a casino are those that have the lowest house advantage.

RULE 6:   Never place a wager in a gambling establishment where the house advantage exceeds 1.5%. This restricts the player to blackjack (properly played), baccarat, and the low percentage bets at craps. In Europe, roulette also becomes a viable game with the single zero wheel and the *"en prison"* feature (wager even money bets only).

RULE 7:   Keep abreast of new developments in gambling—be alert for information that will give you an edge at the tables.

MONEY MANAGEMENT (Chapter 9)

RULE 8:   Never gamble more than you can comfortably afford to lose. Betting "scared" money can adversely affect your play . . . and your life.

RULE 9:   Before you depart for Las Vegas:

(a) Determine how much you intend to gamble. This is your *total gambling stake*.

(b) Determine the number of times you intend to gamble in the casinos. It is recommended that you divide your gambling sessions equally among the days you'll be on your trip.

(c) Budget your total gambling stake over the length of your trip. This is done by dividing the total gambling stake equally among your anticipated gambling sessions. This gives you your per-session stake.

(d) Set winning and losing limits for the total trip *and* individual gambling sessions.

RULE 10:   Once you have established your gambling limits, stick to them at all costs. That goes for your total gambling stake, as well as your per-session stakes. It also includes the winning and losing limits you have set for yourself.

RULE 11: Once you have determined your total trip bankroll, bring only that amount of money with you to Las Vegas. Make sure there is no way you can acquire additional funds for gambling while you are there.

RULE 12: Bring only your allotted stake to each gambling session. Keep any other funds as far away as possible. That way you'll have a margin of safety should your self-control falter.

RULE 13: The size of your wager should be determined by the size of your bankroll at the tables. A bet size that is 2-3% of that bankroll is recommended.

RULE 14: Never increase your bets when losing. Breaking this rule is a surefire ticket to the poorhouse. Don't "steam," or try to chase your losses: a bad losing streak can outlast the financial resources of the richest gamblers.

RULE 15: If you want to bet bigger or more frequently, do so only when you are winning. That way you will be gambling with "casino money."

RULE 16: Play to win...but don't be greedy. As one authority put it: "Don't go for the chandeliers."

RULE 17: If you lose five bets in a row, leave the table at once. This "consecutive loss" rule is designed to get you away from the tables before you lose your temper, and possibly your self-control as well. Nothing is more frustrating to a gambler than a string of losses. Losing time after time is no fun...and it can affect your judgment. So leave and come back later, clear of head and refreshed in spirit.

RULE 18: Don't stay at the tables too long. An hour per session (three or four sessions per day) is about optimal. Playing longer tends to dull your alertness and gives the house percentage more opportunity to work on your bankroll.

RULE 19: Never make a bet to cover costs unrelated to gambling—e.g., dinner, cab fares.

RULE 20: Keep track of all your wagers and make sure your payoffs (from the dealers) are correct.

RULE 21: Take the steps necessary to garage your money in Las Vegas. (See pages 105–110.)

RULE 22: Avoid establishing and utilizing casino credit. Using this type of credit gives the casino management more opportunity to psych you out. When you have ready credit there is always the temptation to use more than you should, even to the point of asking for additional funds once your per-session stake is exhausted. Also, there is the possibility of increasing your credit *ceiling*, a request you might make in the heat of play . . . and regret later on. When you play at the tables, don't sign markers. Bring cash instead . . . it will help keep things in a more realistic perspective.

RULE 23: Don't be afraid to leave Vegas on a moment's notice, if you hit your winning limit for the trip. Remember, you're a winner only when you arrive home with your winnings intact.

HOW TO USE CASINOS EFFECTIVELY
(Chapters 11 & 12)

223

RULE 24: Gamble in casinos that offer you the best chance of winning. These "player-favorable" establishments:
   (a) Play by rules more advantageous to the gambler—for example, permitting double-odds bets at craps;
   (b) Are more "liberal" in their payouts to their customers—returning a higher percentage of the monies wagered on the various casino games;
   (c) Are more tolerant toward players who consistently beat the house;
   (d) Have a psychological atmosphere that helps the gambler win.

RULE 25: Use your *Gambler's Log* (p. 144) and *Casino Locator Checklist* (p.160) to assist you in scheduling play and locating favorable casinos.

RULE 26: Camouflage your winning casino play to avoid harassment by the casino:
   (a) Keep playing sessions short; an hour is ideal.
   (b) If you begin winning big from the outset of a session and you feel casino personnel are getting suspicious of your play...don't hesitate to cut that playing session short.
   (c) Once you complete a session, don't play again until you are in a different casino.
   (d) Use a "round robin" style of play—never gamble in the same casino twice until you've played at every different favorable casino once.
   (e) Try to get casino personnel "on your

side."

(f) Do not make sudden, large changes in the size of your bets.

(g) When interacting with casino personnel, emphasize your losses and play down your wins.

(h) Learn to act like a typical Las Vegas loser.

RULE 27: If you're concerned about being cheated, then gamble *exclusively* in large, successful, legal casinos where the "house" is overwhelmingly honest. As added insurance, don't gamble too long in any one casino, particularly if you are a *consistent* winner.

RULE 28: Get acclimated to the Las Vegas environment before you begin gambling.

RULE 29: Never walk into a gambling establishment on impulse.

RULE 30: Do not spend too much time gambling in a casino (SEE ALSO RULE 18):

(a) Make a gambling itinerary and stick to it. Know in advance when (how often, how long) you're going to be in the casinos. Setting aside specific times for gambling will help you combat the tendency to "lose track" of how long you've been playing.

(b) Make plans to include non-gambling activities in your trip (see Chapter 16). That way you won't end up with time on your hands, get bored, then hit the tables.

(c) Wear a watch and be aware of time. Don't let a clockless city psych you into gambling too long.

RULE 31: When you are winning, it is alright to "toke"

the dealer. Think of the tip as an investment,
an investment in dealer goodwill. This is particularly important in blackjack, where a
dealer can literally "shut a counter down."
Do not, however, tip excessively or to show
off.

RULE 32: Always dispute any casino decision you do
not agree with.

ACHIEVING THE PSYCHOLOGICAL EDGE
(Chapter 13)

RULE 33: Overcome the three psychological governors—negative thinking, Vegas burnout, and
dysfunctional superstitious behavior—that restricts gambling effectiveness and reduces
your chances of winning in games of both
chance and skill.

RULE 34: Take these steps to overcome negative
thinking in the casino:

(a) Understand casino tactics designed to
psych you into losing (Chapters 1-6).

(b) Play "tough." Know the game you are
playing and play it smart. Play only those
games and wagers where you have a
gambling chance of winning (Chapter 8).
Ideally, concentrate on blackjack where
the odds are in *your* favor.

(c) Develop self-control at the tables
(Chapters 9 and 12).

(d) Don't gamble unless you have a *positive
mental attitude*—the belief that you can
win and that you want to win. Do NOT
walk into a casino if you want to lose
(Chapter 6), or if you are a degenerate
gambler (Chapter 18).

RULE 35: Take these steps to overcome Vegas burn-out:

(a) Set up a gambling schedule before you leave on your trip, and stick to it once you arrive in Las Vegas (See also RULE 30a)

(b) Do not gamble more than three or four times a day or more than an hour at a time.

(c) Try not to gamble immediately after you arrive in town—give your body and mind a chance to adjust to the new environment. Also, be wary of "jet lag" if you've just completed a long flight to Las Vegas.

(d) Try to get a reasonable amount of sleep in Las Vegas.

(e) Do not gamble immediately after a heavy meal.

(f) Do not gamble while under the influence of drugs or alcohol.

(g) Do not play when you feel "stale," tired, listless or rundown.

(h) Stop gambling immediately if you feel hassled or emotionally distraught for any reason.

(i) Do not play when you feel sick (even *slightly* sick).

(j) Do not gamble with people who affect your play in a negative manner.

(k) Do not play when you find it difficult to concentrate.

(i) Do not play so long that your senses become dulled.

Look in a mirror before each gambling session. If you appear "wired" or "tired," steer clear of the tables.

(n) Restrict your gambling to casinos that best fulfill your psychological needs (Chapter 12).

(o) Gamble at times when you are mentally *and* physically at your peak. Use your *Body Rhythm Diary* (p. 189) to help determine your peak times.

RULE 36: Do not let superstitious beliefs reduce your playing effectiveness—they can reduce your chances of winning at the tables.

RULE 37: If you're losing during a gambling session, don't become despondent and give up hope. Comebacks are always possible.

RULE 38: If you do lose at a gambling session, put it out of your mind before you gamble again. Each session is a "whole new ballgame," and you should not let previous session experiences affect your current play.

RULE 39: Don't accept casino "freebies," including junkets, if they reduce your gambling effectiveness.

RULE 40: Don't equate money with "macho" at the tables, or forget how much your money is worth in a town that runs on chips and a splurge mentality.

RULE 41: Stay on the psychological offensive. Work at keeping the psychological edge when you gamble in Las Vegas.

A Final Rule and A Final Word About Rules

Perhaps I should add a final personal rule to an already long list—just so you'll see I'm into gambling for enjoyment as well as profit.

RULE 42: Gamble to win *and* have fun.

Let me assure you, I would not gamble if I didn't have fun...there are certainly easier ways to make money! "But," you still might wonder, "how can you enjoy gambling with all those rules to follow?"

I understand this kind of question. I used to bet with total "spontaneity"—there were no rules to be found...anywhere. Such an approach was fun, but it was also costly. As a matter of fact, the reason I first developed a set of playing rules was to see if it would help cut my losses. It did more than that. I found that obeying a set of rules didn't destroy my enjoyment of gambling; to the contrary, it enhanced it. Rules gave structure and meaning to my gambling activities—an orderly, satisfying, winning approach to the tables. So, playing "by the rules" helped me gamble to win *and* have fun.

Please don't assume, however, that the rules in this chapter are "carved on stone tablets." If you want to bend them—even change them—go ahead. As I pointed out earlier in the book, you've got to do what's comfortable for you at the tables. Also, don't assume you must follow these (or any other) rules exactly each time you gamble. I must admit that I don't even follow my own rules all the time, although I win more when I do. I guess there will always be a need for "impulses" and "hunches" in gambling, no matter how scientifically unsatisfying that might be to some of our mathematical friends.

So...should you follow the rules? Here's what I tell myself when the issue arises. The rules in this chapter were designed to give you the best possible chance of winning in the casino. If you choose to alter or ignore them, do so only after you have considered the financial consequences of your actions.

CHAPTER 16

A VICTORIOUS VEGAS VISIT

"In Vegas, you either keep
busy or go broke."
—*Las Vegas Casino Host*

Here are two passages from earlier sections of this book. I want you to read them and tell me what we have:

PASSAGE 1: Don't stay at the tables too long. An hour per day (three or four sessions per day) is about optimal. Playing longer tends to dull your alertness and gives the house percentage more opportunity to work on your bankroll.

PASSAGE 2: Building Vegas in the desert has another advantage, too. It encourages people to gamble more. I mean, what else is there to do in the middle of a town a few miles from Death Valley?

What we have, in essence, is one hell of a problem! First

I tell you to limit your gambling and then I tell you there's not much else to do *but* gamble. What exactly *are* you supposed to do while you're awake in Las Vegas (which for many visitors can run to eighteen hours a day, and longer)? It is imperative that an answer be found: the dream merchants are betting on their desert location to psych you out—hoping it will encourage you to gamble excessively. To gain the psychological edge we've got to find enough activities to keep you occupied and discourage you from spending excessive time at the tables.

Frankly, the longer the time you stay in Vegas, the harder it will be to find non-gambling activities to occupy yourself (how often can you see Hoover Dam!). This becomes a particularly difficult problem for individuals who visit Vegas frequently. Yet, with adequate planning and a healthy dose of imagination, I think we can come up with enough non-gambling activities to help get on the road toward a Victorious Vegas Visit.

How To Find Out About Non-Gambling Activities In Las Vegas

One way is to read the rest of this chapter. In a moment I am going to provide you with a list of various non-gambling activities you can do in and around the city. I believe the list is relatively complete; yet, Vegas is constantly growing and changing—which means that any list will be outdated in a relatively short period of time. Thus, to get a more detailed, up-to-date list of Vegas happenings I recommend you check into:

(1)   *Arthur Frommer's Guide to Las Vegas,*
        which is an excellent source book for ac-

232

tivities in and around the Gambling City (where they are, how to get there, how much they cost). The Guide is normally updated every year or two, so it contains current information.

(2)   The free tabloid newspapers that can be picked up in some hotels and at numerous dispensing racks throughout the city. On a recent trip I picked up the following titles: *Casino Post, Backstage, Las Vegas Mirror, This Week in Las Vegas, Las Vegas Abbey, Vegarama* and *Las Vegas Today.* These tabloids vary in their worth (some are little more than classified ads for sexual services), but some are really excellent sources for current activities in Las Vegas.

The Frommer Guide and the "tabloids" can be used in conjunction with local newspapers and radio & TV reports if you want additional news of Vegas events. You might also try the various visitor "welcome stations" around town, as well as the Las Vegas Convention Bureau.

What You Can Do In Las Vegas...Besides Gamble

If you exclude gambling and a few miscellaneous activities, then what you can do in Las Vegas boils down to the "Five S's:"—

Shows
Shopping
Sports
Sex
Sustenance

not necessarily in that order. Let's examine each one in turn.

Shows: Next to gambling, shows are probably the most popular activity in town. Las Vegas bills itself as "the live entertainment capital of the world," a totally justified title. On any evening you can drive down the Strip and see the names of major entertainers ablaze in neon— entertainers who are making personal appearances in packed hotel showrooms. And they aren't the only shows in town! There are thousands of other performers who participate in the various *production* shows—musicals, plays, variety galas, ice reviews, French follies, etc.

Whether you choose a "name star" or a production show, you won't be disappointed. They are top flight, high energy, lavish events, well worth your time and the expense involved. (Major Strip hotel shows run between $25.00 and $50.00 per person; shows at the smaller hotels can range between $6.00 and $20.00.)

Most hotels have two shows nightly—a dinner show at 8:00, and a cocktail show at midnight. Occcasionally, a third show will be featured at 2:30 am. The dinner show includes a meal in the price of admission and it's normally a few dollars more expensive than the cocktail show, which gives you two or three free drinks. From a financial point of view, the dinner show is a better bargain—but if your budget can afford it, I'd recommend you pass on the dinner shows and save your appetite for the many gourmet restaurants that flourish in Las Vegas. They're too good to miss (see "Sustenance" section, below.)

To give you an idea of the number and variety of shows in Las Vegas, I have included a listing of a typical night's fare in the Gambling City (see Table 16-1). This is an actual guide to major shows that were playing the week of July 10, 1980. The list would be even longer if I had included the various lounge shows which comprise a part of the Vegas entertainment package. These lounge shows are considered "minor" in comparison to the "major" events that take place in the hotel "headliner" rooms, yet in most other cities the entertainers who play them would receive major billing.

TABLE 16-1

A LIST OF MAJOR SHOWS AVAILABLE ON A TYPICAL NIGHT IN LAS VEGAS

HOTEL	SHOW	DESCRIPTION OF SHOW
Aladdin	Wayne Newton	Celebrity
Caesars Palace	Frank Sinatra	Celebrity
Circus Circus	World famous circus acts	Circus acts
Desert Inn	"The Best Little Whorehouse"	Broadway musical
Dunes	"Cabaret de Paris"	French follies
Flamingo	"City Lights"	Spectacular revue
Frontier	"Beyond Belief"	Spectacular revue
Hacienda	"Bottoms Up"	Burlesque revue
Holiday Casino	"The Wild World of Burlesque"	Burlesque revue
Imperial Palace	"Bravo Vegas"	Spectacular revue
Las Vegas Hilton	Bill Cosby	Celebrity
Marina	"Cheek to Cheek"	Topless revue
MGM Grand	Rich Little	Celebrity
Maxim Hotel	"Olde Tyme Burlesque"	Variety
Riviera	Liza Minnelli	Celebrity

HOTEL	SHOW	DESCRIPTION OF SHOW
Royal Casino	"Rare and Bare"	Racy revue
Sahara	Don Rickles	Celebrity
Sands	Glen Cambell	Celebrity
Silver Bird	The 5th Dimension	Musical group
Silver Slipper	"Boy-Lesque"	Female impersonators
Stardust	"Lido de Paris"	French follies
Treasury	"Horsin Around"	Burlesque revue
Tropicana	"Le Follies Bergere"	French follies
Union Plaza	"The Flower Drum Song"	Broadway Kit

In Vegas, there is truly an entertainer for every taste. The following "name stars" were scheduled to appear on Vegas showroom stages in the span of just one summer season: Frank Sinatra, Buddy Hackett, Johnny Carson, Connie Stevens, Robert Goulet, Rodney Dangerfield, Vickie Carr, Cher, Ann Margaret, Bobby Vinton, Barbara Mandrell, Juliet Prowse, Glen Campbell, Paul Anka, Dottie West, Liza Minnelli, Flip Wilson, Vic Damone, Don Rickles, Lola Falana, Bernadette Peters, Tony Bennett, Liberace, Tony Orlando, John Davidson, Donny & Marie, Steve & Eydie, Engelbert, Donna Summer, Captain & Tennille, Rich Little, Lawrence Welk, Mac Davis, Kenny Rogers and Shecky Greene. And this list *doesn't* include the names appearing in Table 16-1!

Don't miss the shows when you're out in Las Vegas. They'll keep your gambling hours down and your spirits up. And remember, you can go to a different show every night of the month and never see the same one twice!

Shopping. Las Vegas is not a town of outstanding malls and department stores. It isn't where you'll find the shopping action, although there is one fine mall (The Boulevard) about a mile from the Strip, and the top quality fashion mall, with major name stores, adjacent to the Frontier Hotel. Rather, it is in the stylish arcades that branch off from the main lobbies of the major Strip hotels where you can find some nice shopping. Here you can lose yourself in hours of delightful browsing among speciality shops and stores which feature the best in merchandise from all over the world. Unfortunately, the shops also feature some of the most outrageous prices this side of Fifth Avenue. . . and there's a reason for this.

To understand why the various arcade shops are so expensive requires an understanding of the clientele they serve. In large part, these stores cater to the "implusive spender" with money to burn—usually a high roller out to impress his companion with a big-ticket gift, and/or a big winner fresh from the tables who is more than willing to pay inflated prices with his new-found wealth.

In one sense these shops are an extension of the "web" I described in Chapter 3. Just when a gambler thinks he's safe—having left the casino with his winnings in hand—he is lured in and trapped by an attractive item in a nearby gift shop. Never mind that it's marked up 200% and more; the gambler buys it without remorse, muttering something like: "What the hell, it's found money," or "If I don't spend it here, I'll just lose it back at the tables." With that kind of an attitude, it's probably better the hapless visitor got the gift. Even though it cost him far more than it was worth. . .at least he'll have something to show for his money when he returns home.

Which is all a long-winded way of saying that I think you will find it's fun to visit the stores and shops in the hotel arcades *as long as you don't do much buying.* If, per chance, you do find a bargain. . .go ahead and make that purchase. Otherwise, be content to note (in memory or on paper) those items you like and then order them through your more reasonably priced stores back home.

Sports. Las Vegas is a very active sports town...thanks in good measure to the construction of *indoor* facilities for various athletic activities. (As I pointed out earlier, who wants to play outdoors and watch their tennis shoes melt?). There is ample opportunity to become a sports participant *or* observer in Vegas, whichever suits your fancy.

For the sports observer, there are several major tournaments to watch—including the Desert Inn Golf Classic, the Mint 400 desert auto race and the Dewar's tennis tournament at the Rivieria. In addition, there are numerous "special events" attractions—like the recent tennis matches and Championship Boxing events sponsored by Caesars Palace. If that isn't enough to keep you occupied, you can visit the MGM to watch Jai Alai; stop by the Silver Slipper for the Wednesday night fights; take in a basketball game at the University; or even attend one of the rodeos that comes through town.

For the sports participant, things get even better. Las Vegas has numerous championship golf courses. (To mention a few: Desert Inn Country Club, Dunes Country Club, Sahara Nevada Country Club, and Tropicana Country Club. Green fees are seasonal, and run around $15.) Vegas also has "more tennis courts open to public play than any city in the world." 37 Many are indoor courts which are lighted for 'round the clock play.

If golf or tennis doesn't interest you, you might want to try bowling at the Showboat Hotel with its 106 lanes and 24-hour a day action. Or maybe you'd prefer to go swimming in one of the huge hotel pools (there are so many swimming pools in Las Vegas that it's affecting the level of humidity in the air!).

There are also deluxe health spas in Las Vegas. Most of the large hotels have them...and they offer everything from saunas and steam baths to weight rooms and massage. Even if you're staying in a smaller hotel or motel, you can still enjoy such luxury facilities by going to a public health club. Consider, for example, the 24-hour, 7-day a week Las Vegas Sporting House. This athletic club advertises twenty-one racquet-ball/handball courts, two squash courts, four platform tennis courts, a completely equipped gymnasium, an indoor jogging track, indoor swimming pool, complete circuit training with nautilus equipment, an outdoor jogging track with parcourse, sun decks, saunas, steam rooms, jacuzzis, massage, and luxurious locker facilities for men and women. Now *that's* a health spa!

Speaking of the Las Vegas Sporting House brings to mind a sporting house of a different kind which leads directly to a discussion of our "fourth S":

Sex. Yes, sex is alive and well in Las Vegas. In fact, when reading some of the adult sections of the free tabloids, you might think it's the number one business in town. Actually, sexual activity in Las Vegas is often overestimated. Many couples who visit the city forego sex in favor of more novel activities they can't do at home. And as far as unattached individuals are concerned—there is more of a tendency to enjoy sexual titillation (e.g., watching scantily-clad cocktail waitresses and half-nude show girls) than to indulge in the real thing.

In fact, Vegas is rampant with sexual exhibitionism, but relatively modest when it comes down to the "nitty-gritty." This is exactly as the dream merchants planned it. They recognize that a sexually charged atmosphere encourages gambling. They also know, however, that when sexual fantasy becomes sexual reality it can reduce gaming revenues. Why? Because it keeps gamblers away from the tables, encouraging them to spend their money in the bedroom rather than in the casino. And that is a no-no in Vegas.

So when it comes to sex in Vegas, it's there for the looking. But when it comes to the taking, well, there's usually a lot less than meets the eye. In fact, it's probably just as easy to obtain commercial sex in most major American cities as it is in Las Vegas, Nevada.

The same can't be said, however, for large segments of Nevada which lie just beyond the boundaries of Clark County. For it is there that the sporting houses of the state are located—houses where sex is the *only* business.

A Nevada bordello is the state's unique contribution to American culture (after all, gambling is now legal in Atlantic City). Nowhere else in the U.S. can you legally visit a house of prostitution and receive sexual favors for a price. And every year thousands of Las Vegas visitors do just that—driving or flying their way to places with names like the "Chicken Ranch" or "Cherry Patch Ranch."*

What's available at such places? Pretty much what you want . . . and can afford. Some brothels come equipped with dungeons where you can be hounded by "dominant," hooded women. Others have special rooms where you can be entertained by several young ladies at once. Running short on cash? You can charge everything on your Visa or MasterCard. Worried about your health? The brothels advertise girls who "have physical inspections." And if you're practical-minded, you'll be pleased to know several houses offer "courtesy gasoline" so you won't get caught with your tank empty.

Finding Nevada brothels can sometimes be a hassle. Although most of them are located near the major roads

(Highway 95, for instance, is referred to as "Whorehouse Highway"), they are not well marked, and unless you know exactly where you're going, you might pass them right by without realizing it.

*If your tastes run more toward voyeurism, there is a total nudity burlesque show at the Palomino Club in North Las Vegas (a few minutes from Casino Center by car).

Those of you interested in the brothel scene might want to pick up a copy of Gerald Paine's *A Bachelor's Guide to the Brothels of Nevada* (Wilmington, Del. Eros Publishing Company). It is carried by the adult bookstores in Las Vegas. The author tells you where the houses are located, what you can expect once you get there, and how much it will cost. A warning, however: brothels, like other businesses, sometimes close and/or relocate. Be sure you establish that the house you want to visit is still in operation before you drive the hour or more it will take to get there.

Sustenance: When it comes to the discussion of food in Las Vegas let me be purposely brief. For its size, Vegas has the best restaurants in the country. Period. And for American cities of *any* size, I'd still place Las Vegas in the top five. That's my opinion . . . but it's backed up with a lot of experience and (unfortunately) weight.

Many people visit Las Vegas all their lives and never realize how good the food really is. This is because they spend most of their time eating at dinner shows and/or the bountiful buffets around town. All this is well and good—the food is satisfactory, plentiful and reasonably priced. But the great food—the *haute-cuisine*—is found elsewhere: in speciality restaurants throughout town and in the gourmet restaurants of the deluxe hotels. To miss out on the gustatory delights that await you in these establishments is like forgetting to take odds on your front line bet. Don't do it!

The next time you go to Vegas, why not make a point of eating at least one meal in a gourmet restaurant? If you're not sure where you want to dine, let me make a recommendation that will simplify things: limit your selection to those gourmet rooms at the deluxe Strip hotels. That way you won't go wrong. Make sure, however, that you get the *gourmet* room, as most major hotels have many restaurants under their roofs. (If you want to make sure you're getting the right place, ask the hotel personnel which restaurant is recommended for their best junket players!) I have always been partial to the gourmet restaurants at the Dunes, Sands, Caesars Palace, and the MGM . . . but there are others which are just as great as well.

Make your reservations when you arrive, as there is limited seating and these fine establishments are in high demand. Sometimes you won't be able to get a reservation on your first-choice day, but usually you'll be able to get one in sometime during your visit (unless, of course, you're a high roller and/or big tipper, at which point you can get in *anywhere* in Vegas).

Most of the gourmet restaurants are open for evening meals only. This "turns off" some people who want to spend most of the night gambling and seeing shows. If you're one of these people, don't despair—there's a simple solution. Make a dinner show reservation in a hotel located near the gourmet restaurant you wish to visit.

Skip the meal at the dinner show and eat at the restaurant instead. You'll have plenty of time to enjoy a truly spectacular meal and still make it to your show before the curtain rises.

* * *

Shows. Shopping. Sports. Sex. Sustenance. Five kinds of activities which are available to you in Las Vegas; things you can do to keep occupied, satisfied, and away from the tables. And there's more. I am now going to list other events you might be interested in—a kind of Las Vegas Directory of Miscellaneous Activities. Please remember that any of these events can change (or be eliminated) over time—so be sure to check their current status when you come to town. The same holds true for out-of-town events I'll be noting. If any interest you, inquire about them from your hotel bellman or at the travel desk when you arrive in Las Vegas. That way you'll get the most up-to-date information concerning transportation to, and costs for, these various events.

Miscellaneous Activities In Las Vegas

Here they are, listed in no particular order. When I have felt the need to comment on any particular activity, I have placed my remarks in parentheses.

★ **Have your photo taken free with the world's most famous gamblers at the Hotel Nevada. (I hope that after you read this book, tourists will be posing with you!)**

★ **Take a sightseeing tour of the city. Several bus trips are available.**

★ **Go to church. They're everywhere in Vegas.**

★ Ice skate at the Ice Palace.

★ See a movie. The MGM has its own theatre where you can sip a cocktail while watching classic movies in the comfort of plush loveseats.

★ Get married. There are no blood test requirements or waiting periods. (Hardly enough time to get you away from the tables.)

★ Visit the Horseshoe's Poker Hall of Fame.

★ Visit the antique slot machine museum at Maxim.

★ Take the "behind the scenes" casino tour at the Mint.

★ Have your picture taken alongside $1 million in cash at the Horseshoe. (Meanwhile, garage your millions and send them home!)

★ Watch television. (You know, the box with the pictures in your hotel room.)

★ Go dancing. (For a nice view, try the 31st floor skytop lounge at the Landmark.)

★ Take a walking tour of the Strip or Casino Center. (Count the lights.)

★ People-watch. (Be subtle.)

★ Attend the Stanley Roberts School of Winning Blackjack. (Before you sit down to play.)

★ Go to conventions around town. (Don't act like you're lost.) If you want a complete list of conventions that will be coming to Las Vegas, you can write the Las Vegas Convention Bureau for a copy.

* * *

Finally, here are a few things to do outside Las Vegas:

★ Visit Death Valley.

★ Take a tour of Hoover Dam.

★ Enjoy the boating and recreational facilities of Lake Mead.

★ Visit Mount Charleston. Hike and camp in the summer; ski (weather permitting) in the winter.
★ See the Grand Canyon. The most spectacular outside-of-Vegas activity available. It's a long distance, so don't underestimate your driving time. You might want to consider taking a tour to the site and/or an airplane trip over the canyon.

Planning Your Victorious Vegas Visit

There you have a whirlwind "what to see and do" tour of the Gambling City and environs. I hope you will find some of the activities interesting enough to pursue during your coming Vegas visit(s). Again, the reason for scheduling non-gambling events on your itinerary is to discourage excessive play at the tables. It's a great way to have a more balanced trip and psych out the dream merchants at the same time.

I find it advantageous to rough out a schedule of activities *before* I leave for Vegas. Nothing final—just enough structure to ward off gambling fever once I arrive. I find that the initial temptation to remain in the casino is reduced if I already have other plans in mind. I think you will, too.

In planning your Vegas trip, why not try the "pick and choose" strategy. First, determine the length of your stay. Then, calculate the number of hours per day you intend to gamble. Once you have these figures, read through the list of things to do in Vegas, "picking and choosing" those activities that interest you. Write them on a separate sheet of paper. Finally, rough out an approximate schedule, assigning times and dates to the various events. Again, this is only a tentative schedule—things can be added, altered or eliminated once you arrive in Nevada. Don't be surprised, however, if your tentative itinerary comes close to reflecting what you actually will do on your trip.

On the following pages I would like to present a "typical itinerary for a three-night, four-day Vegas visit." As you read through the schedule of events, please note that the activities chosen reflect my particular needs and interests. You might select an entirely different set of events. This is fine—select those items that *you'll* enjoy doing.

The only thing you should carry over from my schedule to yours is the emphasis on a limited number of gambling hours per day. If you do limit your gambling, I think you will find your play more satisfying...and more profitable. Nothing is more destructive than staying at the tables until you get bored, bleary-eyed, or busted. Don't let it happen to you!

FIGURE 16-2

A SAMPLE VEGAS TRIP*
Day 1

TIME	ACTIVITY
10:30 a.m.	arrive Las Vegas
11:00	check-in at hotel

*Any time gaps between activities reflect allowances for travel time between events.

TIME	ACTIVITY
11:00-12 noon	unpack and freshen up
12:15- 1:15 p.m.	light lunch
1:30- 2:30	gamble
3:00- 4:00	swim
4:30- 5:30	dress for evening
5:45- 6:45	gamble
7:00- 8:30	dinner (gourmet restaurant)
9:00-10:00	gamble
10:30- 1:30	midnight show
2:00 a.m.+	sleep

Day 2

10:30-11:30 a.m.	breakfast in bed
11:30-12:15 p.m.	shower and dress
12:30- 1:30	gamble
1:45- 2:15	light snack
2:30- 4:00	sports activity (golf, bowling, etc.)
4:15- 5:15	gamble
5:30- 6:00	dress for evening
6:30-10:00	dinner show
10:15-11:15	gamble
11:30-12:00 a.m.	walk (weather permitting)
12:15- 1:15 a.m.	gamble
1:30+	sleep

Day 3

TIME   ACTIVITY

Time	Activity
9:30-10:30 a.m.	breakfast in bed
10:30-11:00	shower and dress
11:15-12:15 p.m.	gamble
12:30- 1:30	light snack
2:00- 3:00	gamble
3:15- 5:15	visit health spa (work out, massage)
5:30- 6:00	dress for evening
6:30- 8:00	dinner, gourmet restaurant
8:00- 8:45	walk (weather permitting)
9:00-10:00	gamble
10:30- 1:30 a.m.	midnight show
2:00- 3:00	gamble (optional, depending on fatigue)
3:15+	sleep

Day 4

Time	Activity
11:00-12:00 noon	shower, dress, pack, check out*
12:15- 1:15	light lunch
1:30- 2:30	gamble
2:30- 3:00	walk (weather permitting)
3:15- 4:15	gamble
5:00- 6:30	dinner (gourmet restaurant)
6:45- 7:45	gamble
8:00-10:00	dinner show (show segment only)
10:15 p.m.	go to airport and await flight

*When you check out, leave your bags with the bell captain and explain you'll be picking them up later in the day. That way you won't have to cart them all over town with you.

Once you get into the swing of planning your Vegas itineraries, you'll find them enjoyable and easy to do. To make your task more successful, I make the following recommendations:

(1) When possible, don't schedule gambling sessions "back to back" (consecutively).

(2) It is helpful to keep physically active during the trip. It keeps the mind and body alert. This is why I like to schedule walks throughout my stay in Las Vegas. (If the weather is bad, you can always walk the corridors of major hotels—many stretch longer than city blocks.)

(3) Avoid scheduling sessions in the casino immediately after you've had a large meal. This can't always be accomplished, but do your best.

(4) Schedule adequate sleeping time into your itinerary. If you normally sleep eight hours a night, then plan for eight hours a night during your trip. I know it is difficult to go to bed in a clockless, pulsating city like Las Vegas—but try to. It will improve your play at the tables (and your disposition, too).

(5) Don't jam too many activities into your day. Give yourself adequate "breathing room." The last thing you want to be is tense and rushed in Las Vegas. I have seen people schedule two—even three—shows in *one* night, and then run all over town trying to keep up with their reservations. Then they try and gamble! It's no wonder they play so frantically...and so badly. Slow down. Don't let the city "wire" you—that's what the dream merchants want.

They say that variety is the spice of life. That's true in Vegas, too. It's not always easy to find variety in the midst of a desert . . . but it is possible, if you work at it. The next time you come to Nevada, make an effort to see something more than the inside of a casino! If you do, you'll improve your chances for enjoyment and winning —and that's what a Victorious Vegas Visit is all about.

CHAPTER 17

RENO, LAKE TAHOE, ATLANTIC CITY—THE WORLD

*"It's been a happy marriage
between me and the Vegas
casinos, but I've been known
to have gambling affairs in
other cities."*
—*A Visiting Las Vegas Gambler*

Throughout this book I have given you tactics to beat the house at its own psychological game and gain that all-important psychological edge at the tables. I have shown you how to use these tactics in psyching out *Vegas* because that city is where most Americans gamble. But, in fact,

the tactics in this book can be used effectively to
gain the psychological advantage in ANY casino
throughout the world.

This is because the playing conditions in legal, well-established, popular gambling casinos are relatively standardized around the globe—and so, too, are the kinds of psychological problems gamblers must overcome if they are to be winners at the tables.

How To Choose a Gambling Casino Outside Of Las Vegas

Playing conditions vary somewhat among casinos in Las Vegas. The same holds true for casinos outside the Gambling City. Thus, before you play in *any* new casino (inside or outside Vegas), you should find out what the establishment's rules and payoffs are for the various games you intend to play, as well as the interaction patterns and psychological atmosphere of that casino. *In other words, you should follow the procedures outlined in Chapter 12 ("How To Choose And Use a Casino").*

If your gambling destination is a long distance away, it is imperative you find this information out *before* you leave...it will mean more effort "up front," but it can sure save a lot of hassles later on. For example, when I first went on a gambling trip to the Bahamas, I failed to check out the rules and payoffs for craps. I paid dearly for this mistake. When I arrived I found that the casino dealt "Eastern style" craps, where no *come* bets are allowed. This is a very unfavorable game for the player...and I ended up not able to play.

If you choose to gamble away from Las Vegas, let me make this recommendation:

Gamble only in those establishments where your chances of winning are as good as in the Vegas casino(s) of your choice.

If you can't find such an establishment where you are (or where you're going), then save your gambling for those places where the chances of winning are good. It will save you money and peace of mind in the long run.*

Gambling In Reno, Lake Tahoe and Atlantic City

To help you determine the kinds of playing conditions you can expect in casinos outside Vegas, let me briefly examine the three other major casino gambling spots in America: Reno, Lake Tahoe and Atlantic City. This information is accurate for the year 1980—but, as you use the information, please keep in mind that casino playing conditions can change over time.

Reno. Gambling in Reno used to be like gambling in downtown Las Vegas: the casual atmosphere, the unpretentious casinos, the decidedly "local" flavor of the patrons who frequented the gaming establishments. That was when Reno was truly the "Biggest Little City in the World." Today, Reno still claims that title, but inevitable expansion has touched this storied western town and turned it into the "Smallest Medium Size City in the World." The good old-fashioned western hospitality is still there, but so are the corporate casino giants, the MGM's of the gambling world.

Reno, in short, is becoming a "two-classed" casino society just like Vegas—you'll find the "Sawdust" joints in the center of the town and the "carpeted" establishment spread out into the city where space is available. Which means that you, the gambler, can select from a wider variety of playing atmospheres than were available a few short years ago.

*If you read *Gambling Times* Magazine regularly you will have the best information available on changing casino rules and conditions around the world.

In fact, there are very few differences today between gambling casinos in Reno and Las Vegas, except that blackjack rules are more favorable in Las Vegas, whereas most places in Reno deal the more favorable, single deck game. Vegas still has a choice of more casinos and casino related entertainment (shows, restaurants, shopping), but Reno has the edge when it comes to outdoor activities and general beauty of the surrounding area. Weather-wise, Reno has the superior climate throughout the late spring, summer and early fall months—but loses the advantage when winter rolls around (unless you happen to prefer colder weather and winter activities). Some individuals like to combine skiing and gambling—and if this is your choice, I'd recommend you pass up Reno and get closer to the slopes in:

Lake Tahoe. This is truly one of the most beautiful gambling spots in the world, and ideal for the player who is also an outdoorsman. The gambling resorts nestled in the pines along the South Shore of Lake Tahoe provide the visitor with easy access to a clear alpine lake, fantastic mountain-skiing (Winter Olympics were held in nearby Squaw Valley), scenic western towns (e.g., Virginia City), and historic sights.

Several "major name" casinos are located in the Lake Tahoe area—but not in the numbers found in Las Vegas or even Reno. This means that your choice of places to gamble (and enjoy casino-related entertainments) is limited; fortunately, however, playing conditions are the same as in Reno.

Many gamblers choose to shuttle between Reno and Lake Tahoe for their gambling and sightseeing activities. Except in the snowy winter months, this is a relatively easy option to exercise . . . and should give you a full complement of casinos in which to ply your gaming skills.

Atlantic City. Whenever I think of this newest casino

gambling spot I'm reminded of the line from an old song: "Our day will come." This is probably true for Atlantic City, but that day isn't quite here yet (at least not in 1982 when this chapter was written).

Atlantic City is a promise waiting to be fulfilled, and until it is fulfilled, I cannot recommend it as strongly as Vegas for your gambling activity. This is not because the casino managers or town fathers have done something wrong—it is simply because there are still problems Atlantic City must work out before playing conditions and competition between casinos make gaming worthwhile from the player's point of view.

(Just prior to this printing, Atlantic City made the game of blackjack even less worthwhile to play by eliminating the "surrender" rule. Formerly, the use of "surrender," especially "early surrender," gave the player an advantage at "21" he can no longer enjoy in New Jersey.)

Every time I have been to Atlantic City I have confronted negative casino conditions like these:
(1) Crowds so thick at the tables, you couldn't gamble comfortably. Sometimes you couldn't even find a seat open at the lower-limit tables.
(2) Only a limited number of casinos in operation (9), giving the player less choice of playing conditions and atmospheres—and making "round-robin" play more difficult.
(3) Rules in some games not as favorable to the player as in Vegas, Reno and Lake Tahoe. (Example: Only two casinos offer double odds on craps . . . and this offer is a very recent innovation.)

(4) The rule, in some casinos, is that you must wear a dinner jacket in the evening. This is a ridiculous rule, aimed at making the casino a "class" operation. All it succeeds in doing is making some gamblers uncomfortable in the hot and stuffy atmosphere of an overcrowded casino.

(5) Limited and costly parking.

(6) The feeling that you are gambling in the middle of a slum. (Which, of course, is true.) With redevelopment well under way in Atlantic City, this might not be a problem in the future; but right now the areas surrounding the casinos are eyesores.

(7) A very limited entertainment calendar.

Of course, there is the beach—usable part of the year—but otherwise the non-gambling activity in the 1982 schedule is bleak. Right now, there isn't much else to do in Atlantic City but gamble. . . and that is a dangerous condition for the player who wants the psychological edge in his battle against the casino.

During my last visit to Atlantic City I spotted an advertisement for a casino show that said it all: "Come see our Las Vegas style revue," the sign proclaimed. Better yet, why not go to Vegas and see it? You'll be better off all the way around. . . at least until Atlantic City comes of age as a gambling town.

Gambling Outside The United States

One thing about gambling—it enjoys an international popularity. Many countries have their own casinos, some of them quite delightful and favorable for the player. I have always enjoyed, for example, the casinos in London—they have that certain British aristocratic charm...and the playing conditions are favorable.

Yet, when it comes to gambling in general, I prefer to spend most of my time in American casinos. This goes beyond the spirit of patriotism...when it comes to issues of money and gambling, I want to be in a place where I am sure of my rights and of my rights to demand them. I wouldn't be at all surprised if a Frenchman felt that way about French casinos, or a German about German gambling establishments.

This opinion of mine is admittedly a highly personal one, and not one that you should feel obligated to follow. Unlike other recommendations I make in this book, you might ignore this one and still be a top flight winner in the psychological battle with the casino. All I ask you to do—if you choose to gamble in casinos outside of the United States—is to be sure of the local rules and casino conditions before you play...and to be sure to follow *all customs or rules in the foreign countries you visit.*

CHAPTER 18

A PERSONAL NOTE TO
THE DEGENERATE GAMBLER

> "To make a mistake is
> human. To learn from it is
> wisdom."
> —*Anonymous*

I started this book with a gambling story. Let me end it the same way.

The Beginnings Of Wisdom

Most people who visit Las Vegas come to gamble. "Dr. K" came to get a divorce. For six weeks he lived in the Gambling City, establishing residence and a growing affection for the crap tables. By the time he left Nevada to return East, he had gone from a hesitant $1.00 bettor to an aggressive $5.00 "splurger."

Over the next few years, Dr. K's gambling appetite grew and he made several return trips to Vegas. As he began edging toward higher bets and faster action, casino personnel started taking a personal interest in his play. They offered him "freebies," including junkets. He established a credit line and began playing off markers. The trips became more frequent, and more costly.

Dr. K became a "steamer" at the dice tables. When he was winning, things were fine; but when he fell behind, he'd "chase his losses"—increasing his bets and dropping a bundle. There were some trips when he'd fly out for a five-day junket, but end up returning home the same day...flat broke.

Things were getting out of hand; yet, when Dr. K was asked if he had a gambling problem, he would answer "no"...and believe it. It took a financial debacle and a huge one-year loss at the tables to finally convince Dr. K that he was, indeed, a degenerate gambler. For two years he gave up gambling completely, vowing never to return to Vegas unless he could bring his gambling under control.

Now here's a question some of you may be pondering: How did I come to know so much about the gambling career of "Dr. K"? *Because I am Dr. K.* And what I learned about losing can help you be a winner.

A Psychologist Looks At Himself

When I finally realized I had a gambling problem I decided to take a good, long look at myself. After all, I was a trained psychologist; if I couldn't understand my behavior, who could? What I discovered wasn't exactly ego-boosting: the major reason I lost at the tables was not due to the house percentage but, rather, the house *psychology*. The irony was not lost on me. I, a professional psychologist, had been psyched out at the tables.

I felt like a hunter who had been shot with his own gun. There was no getting around it—I had fallen victim to the dream merchants' hype, and had given Vegas a whopping psychological edge at the tables.

So much for the bad news. The good news is that once I realized that psychological factors were primarily responsible for my downfall, I was in an excellent position (because of my training) to turn things around and use these factors to my advantage. Keeping the "hunter" analogy, now I could grab hold of the dream merchants' "big gun"—the psychological ploy—and turn it on them.

Understanding how I lost helped me understand how to win. It enabled me to identify and counter the dream merchants' tactics. Now it was my turn to go on the psychological offensive—to psych out Vegas and ensure myself the psychological edge at the tables. The strategy I developed and utilized became the subject matter of this book.

The strategy worked for me. And now that you know how to psych out Vegas, it should work for you, too.

I can say one thing with certainty: if you follow the gambling procedures I have set forth you will not—you *cannot*—gamble in a degenerate manner. You can't because my entire strategy is predicated on a set of playing rules which makes it impossible to gamble at a psychological disadvantage. Remember, I developed these rules to stop *myself* from gambling in a degenerate manner.

Let me repeat—if you follow my recommendations you will gamble from a position of psychological strength. You *will* psych out Vegas and you *will* keep the psychological advantage on your side of the table.

But what if you can't—or won't—follow my recommendations? Does that mean you're a degenerate gambler? Not necessarily (you might just be stubborn!). But if you balk at my suggestions and also exhibit some or all of the following characteristics—then your chances of being (or becoming) a degenerate gambler are pretty high.

Some Characteristics Of Degenerate Gamblers

(1) Gambling becomes the focal point of that person's life.

(2) Although he might not admit it or understand why, the major goal of the degenerate gambler is not to win, but to stay in the action.

(3) Money for gambling takes precedence over money for almost any other purpose.

(4) The degenerate gambler tends to remember his wins and forget his losses.

(5) The degenerate gambler tends to deny or ignore just how bad his financial condition has become as a result of his habit.

(6) A degenerate gambler is usually the last person to find out about his condition. He is like the alcoholic who "doesn't have a drinking problem."

(7) The degenerate gambler will go to great lengths to get playing capital—he'll borrow from friends, family, banks. With truly sick cases, the gambler will steal or embezzle monies to feed his habit.

(8) The degenerate gambler will often lie about the extent of his habit.

(9) The degenerate gambler is always talking about a "lucky streak" that's just around the corner. He also justifies gambling losses by pointing out the

"entertainment value" of his "investment."

(10) The degenerate gambler will often "quit" his habit after a big loss—only to return to the tables when the urge for action becomes too compelling for him to resist.

(11) Contrary to popular belief, a person can be a degenerate gambler and bet on only one type of game.

What Should You Do If You're a Degenerate Gambler?

Your course of action is clear. Either overcome your affliction, or stop gambling altogether. I know that sounds harsh. It's meant to. The degenerate gambler has a powerful addiction. It can destroy him emotionally as well as financially. No gambling is worth *that*.

Please recall my earlier observation: it is vital that each of you accurately and honestly assess your own gambling behavior—determine for yourself whether you can control your play at the tables. If, after reading this book, you decide you cannot control your gambling . . . then you will have to eliminate Las Vegas from your life.

If you enjoy gambling as much as I do, then that kind of a decision will be one of the most difficult you will ever make. Yet, it is a decision which must be made if you are to ensure your financial survival and self-esteem. Remember that, at one point in my life, I was faced with just such a decision . . . and had I not been able to psych out the dream merchants and get my gambling under control, I would have been forced to leave Las Vegas forever.

AFTERWORD

Whenever I go to Vegas I look forward to the experience—not just in terms of winning, but also as an opportunity to sharpen my psychological strength against the juggernaut casinos.

Winning the psychological battle against the dream merchants is important to me. It gives me the psychological advantage not only in the casino, but anywhere that mental power is needed. As strange as it may seem, a casino is an excellent place to develop mental resolve, to learn psychological self-control under fire. After all, if you can resist the temptations of Las Vegas...what mountain can't you climb?

The next time you hit Vegas, plunge into the psychological fray with all guns blazing! Gain the psychological edge and you'll have your gambling chance of winning...in all of life's little games.

APPENDIX A

YOU CAN MAKE BOOK ON THESE

> "Knowledge and human
> power are synonymous."
> —*Francis Bacon*

Knowledge is a powerful weapon you can use in your battle to psych out Vegas. Here are a few reading selections to help you gain the psychological advantage at the tables.

Suggested Reading

(1) Ainslie, Tom. *How to Gamble in a Casino*. New York; William Morrow & Co., 1979.

A well-written, no-nonsense introduction to casino gambling for those who vacation in places like Las Vegas and Atlantic City.

(2) Andersen, Ian. *Turning the Tables on Las Vegas*. New York; Vanguard Press, 1976.

A complete introduction to effective blackjack play. A valuable discussion on the need for camouflage at the tables, and how to accomplish it. A good chapter on poker is also included.

(3) Braun, Julian. *How to Play Winning Blackjack*. Chicago; Data House, 1980.

A clear, easy-to-understand presentation of a professional level blackjack strategy by one of the pioneers in the field. An intellectually honest book.

(4) Brunson, Doyle. *Super/System—A Course in Power Poker*. Gardena, CA; B & G Publishing, 1980.

Previously titled *How I Made Over $1,000,000 Playing Poker*. The bible for professional poker players, and it's a must for the serious poker student. An encyclopedia of more than 600 pages of detailed strategy.

(5) Canfield, Richard A. *Blackjack Your Way to Riches*. Secaucus, NJ; Lyle Stuart Inc., 1979.

An interesting book written by a former pit boss in association with others. Features playing against the shoe, modification of basic strategy, players' styles, and just about everything connected with blackjack.

(6) Fisk, M.C. *The Gambler's Bible*. New York; Drake Publishers, 1976.

This book covers everything from harness racing to betting on presidential elections. Casino gambling comprises 25% of the text.

(7) Friedman, Bill. *Casino Games*. New York; Golden Press, 1973.

A "learn-by-seeing" approach to casino gambling. Numerous photos and illustrations. Good for the beginner. Covers blackjack, craps, roulette, baccarat and keno.

(8) Friedman, Bill. *Casino Management*. Secaucus, NJ; Lyle Stuart Inc., 1982.
Know your enemy! This book will help. A very valuable inside look at all phases of casino operation. Don't miss this one!

(9) "Gambling Times" staff. *Big Winner's System Book*. Los Angeles; Gambling Times, 1981.
Offers the reader 48 all-inclusive gambling systems and betting methods published during the past seven years. Features craps, blackjack, roulette, horse racing, sports handicapping, keno and a sprinkling of others.

(10) Hutchens, John K. *The Gambler's Bedside Book*. New York; Taplinger Publishing Co., 1977.
A collection of delightful stories and essays about gamblers and gambling. Go ahead and take it to bed with you!

(11) Patterson, Jerry. *Blackjack's Winning Formula*. Vorhees, NJ; Echelon Press, 1977.
This book covers basic strategy for playing in Nevada, Atlantic City and the Caribbean.

(12) Puzo, Mario. *Inside Las Vegas*. New York; Charter Books, 1979.
A famous writer who is also a gambler gives us an intimate view of a city he loves. A wealth of information and advice...from a man who knows of what he speaks.

(13) Renzoni, Tommy. *Renzoni on Baccarat*. Secaucus, NJ; Lyle Stuart Inc., 1973.
A discussion of baccarat by the man who brought the game to American casinos. Features fundamentals, rules and strategy advice.

(14) Roberts, Stanley. *Winning Blackjack*. Los Angeles;

SRS Enterprises, 1981.

Straightforward, informative blackjack strategy from the man who founded a national chain of blackjack schools. A valuable primer for the serious "21" player. Expensive, but well worth it.

(15) "Rouge et Noir" staff. *Winning at Casino Gambling*. Glen Head, NY; Rouge et Noir, Inc., 1966.

A how-to book written by experienced gamers, this is considered a virtual encyclopedia. Certain sections are dated, but otherwise it's still applicable.

(16) Scarne, John. *Scarne's New Complete Guide to Gambling*. New York; Simon & Schuster, 1974.

A truly exhaustive work. Scarne has been on the gambling scene for many years, and happens to be an expert magician as well as an expert player.

(17) Scarne, John. *Scarne on Dice*. New York; Crown Publishers, 1980.

A detailed discussion of casino craps and other dice games. There's a very interesting section on dice "cheaters" and their moves.

(18) Silberstang, Edwin. *How to Gamble and Win*. New York; Cornerstone Library, 1980.

Another gambling authority does a nice job of presenting gambling information. Emphasis is placed on craps, blackjack, poker, sports betting and the horses.

(19) Sklansky, David. *Sklansky on Poker Theory*. Las Vegas; Gambler's Book Club, 1976.

A successful and active Las Vegas poker professional reveals his secrets. Also by the same author: *Hold 'Em Poker*.

(20) Snyder, Arnold. *Blackjack for Profit: A Guidebook*

for Card Counters. Berkeley, CA; R.G. Enterprises, 1982.

The book is based on The Blackjack Formula. It's considered basic survival information for players with limited bankrolls. Compares 18 different systems and their profitability.

(21) Stuart, Lyle. *Casino Gambling for the Winner*. Secaucus, NJ; Lyle Stuart Inc., 1978.

A high-rolling gambler reveals his approach to winning baccarat and craps. Entertaining and informative and reads like fiction. Includes comments on slots and keno.

(22) Thorp, Edward O. *Beat the Dealer: A Winning Strategy for the Game of Twenty-One*. New York; Random House, 1966.

This is the book that started it all and forced the casinos in Nevada to change the rules of "21." The book is outdated, but still is enlightening reading.

(23) Wilson, Allan N. *Casino Gambler's Guide*. New York; Harper & Row, 1970.

This is my favorite "introductory text." It is more difficult than most, but a real gem! Absolutely "must" reading for the serious gambler.

(24) Winkless, N.B. *The Gambling Times Guide to Craps*. Secaucus, NJ; Lyle Stuart, 1983.

Here's how to talk craps language, how to reckon the odds and payoffs, how well systems do, and how to play and enjoy the game.

(25) Uston, Ken. *Million Dollar Blackjack*. Secaucus, NJ; Lyle Stuart Inc., 1982.

Uston is considered the world's greatest blackjack player by most gaming experts. The book offers something for virtually every level of play, from beginner to super-advanced. Contains his advanced point count system and covers front-loading, spooking, and cheating from both sides of the table.

(26) *WIN* Magazine.

Now in its 12th year, this nationally-circulated publication brings its readership the most comprehensive information on every facet of legal gambling. The only consumer-oriented publication of its kind, *WIN* is gambling's publication of record and offers the insights of the top movers and shakers in the gaming realm. Each month its expert staff provides the gaming consumer with a valuable "winner's edge" through articles on the latest and best casino, sports betting and handicapping systems. Each month, *WIN* casts special light on the world's newest and most luxurious gaming resort hotels and takes you inside the corporate boardrooms to chart the trends and future of the gaming industry. International in scope, *WIN* travels the globe to unearth all the latest developments on the international gambling scene. Gamblers call *WIN* "the best, most up-to-date gambling reference available anywhere." The subscription price is $36 per year.

(27) *The Experts Blackjack Newsletter.*

Published bimonthly, this newsletter for the serious blackjack player features systems and strategies from today's top professionals. An in-house journal for the fraternity of winning "21" players, this publication provides a timely overview of playing conditions at blackjack tables from Atlantic City to Las Vegas and Reno/Tahoe to Laughlin. Opinionated and contentious, the newsletter pulls no punches in bringing the discriminating blackjack devotee strategic up-to-the-moment data on where to find the best playing conditions in regard to shuffle depth, number of decks, countermeasures, treatment of card counters, existence of favorable or unfavorable house rules and betting limits. This Gambling Times Inc. product is simply The Unrivaled Bible of Blackjack. Yearly subscription price is $30 for 6 issues.

272

APPENDIX B

FOOTNOTES

1. *Winning at Casino Gaming* (Glen Head, New York: Rouge Et Noir, Inc., 1966), p. 8.

2. Mario Puzo, *Inside Las Vegas* (New York: Charter Books, 1979), p. 22.

3. A great description of this stimulus bombardment and its impact is provided by Tom Wolfe in his article, "Las Vegas (What?) Las Vegas (Can't hear you! Too noisy) Las Vegas!!!!," reprinted in John K. Hutchens (ed.), *The Gambler's Bedside Book* (New York; Taplinger Publishing Co., 1977), pp. 73-81.

4. Ian Andersen, *Turning the Tables on Las Vegas* (New York: Vanguard Books, 1976), p. 3.

5. Bill Friedman, *Casino Management* (Secaucus, New Jersey: Lyle Stuart, Inc., 1974), p. 23.

6. Mario Puzo, *Inside Las Vegas,* p. 147.

7. This story—and others like it—comes from Lyle Stuart's *Casino Gambling for the Winner* (Secaucus, New Jersey: Lyle Stuart, Inc., 1978).

8. *Winning at Casino Gaming,* pp. 258-259.

9. A similar incident is reported by John Savage, in *The Winner's Guide to Dice* (New York: Charter Books, 1974), p. 7.

10. Mario Puzo, *Inside Las Vegas,* p. 210.

11. As reported in Lyle Stuart's *Casino Gambling for the Winner,* p. 165.

12. Ian Andersen, op. cit, pp. 3-4.

13. Mario Puzo, op. cit, p. 72.

14. Tommy Renzoni, *Baccarat* (Secaucus, New Jersey: Lyle Stuart, 1973), pp. 64-65.

15. Morris Renek, *Las Vegas Strip* New York: Avon Books, 1975), p. 216.

16. Tommy Renzoni, *Baccarat,* pp. 97-98.

17. Allan N. Wilson, *The Casino Gambler's Guide* (New York; Harper & Row, 1965), p. 8.

18. Lyle Stuart, op. cit, p. 13.

19. I am assuming, of course, that the casino will accept your bet...which will not happen if your wager is greater than the house limit. In some casinos, however, the house limit exceeds $10,000 on a *pass line* craps wager (with odds...and for many people that is more money than they'll ever want to wager!).

20. This does not hold true for expert play at blackjack...where the player can gain the mathematical edge.

21. An excellent discussion of "bet sizing" appears in Allan Wilson's *The Casino Gambler's Guide* (Chapter 17).

22. Allan Wilson, pp. 207-208.

23. Ibid, p. 275.

24. John Scarne, *Scarne on Dice* (New York: Crown Publishers, 1980), p. 266.

25. Mike Goodman and Michael J. Goodman, *Your Best Bet* (Northridge, California: Brooke House, 1975), p. 77.

26. Ibid, p. 138.

27. Stanley Roberts, "Casino Blackjack: An Unsporting Proposition" (*Gambling Times,* August, 1979), p. 13.

28. Ian Andersen, op. cit., pp. 133-134.

29. Ibid, p. 34. The author presents an excellent table showing you how to camouflage your play at the chart.

30. Ibid, p. 95.

31. Mario Puzo op. cit. p. 102.

32. Lyle Stuart, op. cit. p. 107.

33. Len Miller, "Gambling in London" *(Gambling Times,* August, 1979), p. 34.

34. Bill Friedman, *Casino Management,* pp. 45-46.

35. B. Ottum, "Hoodoo? Well, He Do," *(Sports Illustrated,* March 8, 1971), p. 11.

36. From the December, 1980 issue of *Gambling Times* Magazine.

37. Arthur Frommer, *Arthur Frommer's Guide to Las Vegas* (New York: Frommer/Pasmantier Pub. Corp., 1979), p. 2.

KEEPING YOUR GAMING KNOWLEDGE CURRENT THROUGH *WIN*

You can successfully control your gaming behavior and turn a losing attitude into a lifetime winning streak by keeping abreast of the continuous changes and developments in legalized gambling. *WIN* Magazine (formerly *Gambling Times*) can give you that information.

Since February of 1977, readers of *WIN* Magazine (formerly *Gambling Times)* have profited immensely. They have done so by using the information they have read each month. if that sounds like a simple solution to winning more and losing less, well it is! Readers look to *WIN* for that very specific reason. And it delivers.

WIN is totally dedicated to showing readers how to win more money in every form of legalized gambling. How much you're going to win depends on many factors, but it's going to be considerably more than the cost of a subscription.

WINNING AND MONEY

Winning, that's what *WIN* is all about. And money, that's what *WIN* it all about. Because winning and money go hand in hand.

Here's what the late Vince Lombardi, the famous football coach of the Green Bay Packers, had to say about winning:

"It's not a sometime thing. Winning is a habit. There

277

is no room for second place. There is only one place in my game and that is first place. I have finished second twice in my time at Green Bay and I don't ever want to finish second again. The objective is to win—fairly, squarely, decently, by the rules—but to win. To beat the other guy. maybe that sounds hard or cruel. I don't think it is. It is and has always been an American Zeal to be first in anything we do, and to win, and to win and to win.''

Mr. Lombardi firmly believed that being a winner is ''man's finest hour.'' *WIN* believes it is too, while being a loser is depressing, ego-deflating, expensive and usually very lonely. ''Everybody loves a winner'' may be a cliche, but it's true. Winners command respect and are greatly admired. Winners are also very popular and have an abundance of friends. You may have seen a winner in a casino, with a bevy of girls surrounding him...or remember one who could get just about any girl he wanted.

Some of the greatest gamblers in the world also have strong views on what winning is all about. Here's what two of them have to say on the subject:

> ''To be a winner, a man has to feel good about himself and know he has some kind of advantage going in. I never made bets on even chances. Smart is better than lucky.''
> —''Titanic'' Thompson

> ''When it comes to winnin', I got me a one-track mind. You gotta want to win more than anything else. And you gotta have confidence. You can't pretend to have it. That's no good. You gotta have it. You gotta know. Guessers are losers. Gamblin's just as simple as that.''
> —Johnny Moss

WIN will bring you the knowledge you need to come home a winner and come home in the money. For it is knowledge, the kind of knowledge you'll get in its pages, that separates winners from losers. It's winning and money that *WIN* offers you. *WIN* will be your working manual to winning wealth.

The current distribution of this magazine is limited to selected newsstands in selected cities. Additionally, at newstands where it is available, it's being snapped up, as soon as it's displayed, by gamblers who know a sure bet when they see one.

So if you're serious about winning, you're best off subscribing to *WIN*. Then you can always count on its being there, conveniently delivered to your mailbox—and what's more, it will be there one to two weeks before it appears on the newsstands. You'll be among the first to receive the current issue as soon as it comes off the presses, and being first is the way to be a winner.

Having every monthly issue of *WIN* will enable you to build an "Encyclopedia of Gambling," since the contents of this magazine are full of sound advice that will be as good in five or ten years as it is now.

As you can see, a subscription to *WIN* is your best bet for a future of knowledgeable gambling. It's your ticket to *WINNING* and *MONEY*.

Take the time to read the following offer. As you can see, *WIN* has gone all out to give you outstanding bonuses. You can join the knowledgeable players who have learned that *WIN* helps them to win more money.

NINE NEW WAYS TO GET 12 WINNING ISSUES OF *WIN* FREE...

Every month over 250,000 readers trust *WIN* to introduce powerful new winning strategies and systems. Using proven scientific methods, the world's leading experts show you how to win big money in the complex field of gambling.

WIN has shown how progressive slot machines can be beaten. Readers have discovered important new edges in blackjack. They've been shown how to know for sure when an opponent is bluffing at poker. *WIN* has also spelled out winning methods for football, baseball and basketball. They've published profound new ways of beating horses. Their team of experts will uncover information in the months

279

ahead that's certain to be worth thousands of dollars to you.

In fact, the features are so revolutionary that they must take special precautions to make sure *WIN* readers learn these secrets long before anyone else. So how much is *WIN* worth to you? Well...

NOW *WIN* CAN BE BETTER THAN FREE! Here's how: This BONUS package comes AUTOMATICALLY TO YOU WHEN YOU SUBSCRIBE...or goes to a friend if you give a gift subscription.

★1.   A CARD that entitles you to a 50% discount at over 2,000 quality hotels in over 400 cities, mainly in North America and the Caribbean. Only the finest hotels are included; chains such as Holiday Inn, Sheraton, Hilton, Best Western, Marriott and Ramada Inns. Discounts are good 365 days per year. Stay as long as you like, subject to availability. Save as much as $100 per night.

★2.   A 50% discount on a one week stay in over 2,000 condominiums, worldwide, including the United States, Canada, Mexico, France, Bahamas, Jamaica, Italy, Spain, Germany, Austria, Aruba and many more! Reservations made by a toll free number.

★3.   Free Kodak film for life when you use our specified National Processing laboratory, which gives a 40% discount off Kodak list prices for developing. Free Kodak Color film, any size, speed or exposure to fit your camera, is provided with each roll of film developed.

★4.   A 5% REBATE on the lowest available scheduled Airline fares in the US and up to a 45% REBATE on international flights when you book through our contract agency, San Diego Travel. Licensed and Bonded since 1963. Reservations can be made by a toll free number.

★5.   A 3 day/2 night FREE vacation for two in your choice of Las Vegas, Reno, Tahoe, Atlantic City or Hawaii, plus Disneyland or DisneyWorld—when you book your air fare and reservations through our travel agency, San Diego Travel.

★6.   A funpack booklet entitling the holder to over $250 in discounts at local businesses in your choice of: Las Vegas, Reno, Tahoe, Atlantic City, Hawaii, Orlando, Carlsbad-Oceanside, Disneyland, Palm Springs or Acapulco, Mexico. Includes cash, meals, chips, Keno, lucky bucks, slot tokens, drinks, entertainment, attractions and much, much more! Outside of Nevada the funpack may not include cash or gambling benefits. Good 7 days a week, including all holidays.

★7. 15% to 50% discounts on over 1,000 cruise trips. Savings can be as much as $1,000 per cruise. Includes a $50 per cabin bar-boutique ship credit. Reservations by toll free number.

★8. A standard discount on car rental from Hertz, Avis, Budget and Alamo car rental agencies. Guaranteed lowest prices, not available to the public. Toll free numbers in US & Canada.

★9. Your choice of a FREE 3-piece, 6-piece or all 9-piece set of English Leather Designer Luggage. Total value of all 9 pieces is $199.90. Gift certificate with each subscription.

To begin your delivery of *WIN* magazine at once, enclose a payment of $36.00 by check or money order (U.S. currency), Mastercard or Visa. Add $5.00 per year for postage outside the United States. Send payment to:

WIN MAGAZINE
16760 Stagg St., Suite 213
Van Nuys, CA 91406-1642

Other Valuable Sources of Knowledge Available Through *Gambling Times Inc.*

The following publications and books are available through Gambling Times Inc., 16760 Stagg St., Suite 213, Van Nuys, CA 91406.

The Experts Blackjack Newsletter.
This bi-monthly newsletter has all the top blackjack Experts working just for you. Features answers, strategies and insights that were never before possible. Yearly subscription price is $30 for 6 issues.

Winning by Computer
by Dr. Donald Sullivan

SPORTS BETTING BOOKS
Fast Track to Thoroughbred Profits
by Mark Cramer
The GT Guide to Basketball Handicapping
by Barbara Nathan
The GT Guide to Football Handicapping
by Bob McCune
The GT Guide to Greyhound Racing
by William McBride
The GT Guide to Harness Racing
by Igor Kusyshyn, Ph.D., Al Stanley
and Sam Dragich
The GT Guide to Jai Alai
by William R. Keevers
The GT Guide to Thoroughbred Racing
by R.G. Denis